The Complete Guide to Chair Caning

The Complete Guide

to Chair Caning

RESTORING CANE, RUSH, SPLINT, WICKER & RATTAN FURNITURE

by Jim Widess

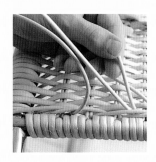

LARK BOOKS

A Division of
Sterling Publishing Co., Inc.
New York

Library of Congress Cataloging-in-Publication Data

Widess, Jim.
 The complete guide to chair caning : restoring cane, rush, splint, wicker,
and rattan furniture / by Jim Widess.-- 1st ed.
     p. cm.
 Includes bibliographical references and index.
 ISBN 1-57990-613-3 (hardcover)
 1. Chair caning. I. Title.
TT199.W53 2006
684.1'3--dc22

                                        2005014621

10 9 8 7 6 5 4 3 2 1

First Edition

Published by Lark Books, A Division of
Sterling Publishing Co., Inc.
387 Park Avenue South, New York, N.Y. 10016

Text © 2005, Jim Widess
Photography © 2005, Jim Widess unless otherwise specified
Illustrations © 2005, Lark Books

Distributed in Canada by Sterling Publishing,
c/o Canadian Manda Group, 165 Dufferin Street
Toronto, Ontario, Canada M6K 3H6

Distributed in the U.K. by Guild of Master Craftsman Publications Ltd., Castle
Place, 166 High Street, Lewes, East Sussex, England BN7 1XU
Tel: (+ 44) 1273 477374, Fax: (+ 44) 1273 478606, e-mail: pubs@thegmc-
group.com, Web: www.gmcpublications.com

Distributed in Australia by Capricorn Link (Australia) Pty Ltd.,
P.O. Box 704, Windsor, NSW 2756 Australia

If you have questions or comments about this book, please contact:
Lark Books
67 Broadway
Asheville, NC 28801
(828) 253-0467

Manufactured in China

ISBN 13: 978-1-57990-613-9
ISBN 10: 1-57990-613-3

For information about custom editions, special sales, premium and corporate
purchases, please contact Sterling Special Sales Department at 800-805-5489 or
specialsales@sterlingpub.com.

Editor:
James Knight

Art Director:
Kristi Pfeffer

Cover Designer:
Barbara Zaretsky

Assistant Editor:
Rebecca Guthrie

Associate Art Director:
Shannon Yokeley

Editorial Assistance:
Delores Gosnell

Art Production:
Jeff Hamilton

Editorial Intern:
David Squires

Contents

"I was teaching elementary school when I caned my first chair. Those nine hours afforded me the time to think about something other than usual daily concerns. It was a totally freeing experience. Completing the job in just a few hours, having it look good, and hearing people's reactions gave me great satisfaction. It was an immensely positive experience. Caning that first chair changed my life."

—Jim Widess

Introduction

Not long ago, people discarded household items if they became broken or slightly out of vogue. Nowadays, people have a renewed appreciation for original classics, and many have discovered the joy of restoring them to their former glory.

Maybe you have an old chair that has a torn cane seat. Perhaps there's a wicker table hidden in your basement that needs tightening and its joins rewrapped. With a little help, things like these can once again become useful additions to a room or centerpieces of timeless grace and elegance. This book can show you how to do it. It describes the materials, tools, and techniques you'll need to know to fix almost any piece of cane or wicker furniture. So whether you have a Victorian cane-bottomed chair, a contemporary rattan magazine rack, or a Depression-era footstool in need of a new splint cover, you'll be able to fix it with help from easy-to-understand instructions and hundreds of step-by-step photographs.

Because no two pieces of furniture are exactly alike, *The Complete Guide to Chair Caning* provides insights, tips, and techniques you can modify and use for your own projects. You'll learn about the decorative versatility of pre-woven cane, hand-caning techniques, rush and splint weaving, wicker repair, and rattan wraps through hands-on experience that will give you a complete toolbox of furniture caning know-how for the future.

Beginners Welcomed

Don't shy away from trying a caning project just because the design may look intricate or complex. In fact, the secret to successful chair caning is this: simple steps build to produce a dazzling final work of art that is both beautiful and functional. To top it off, caning is incredibly forgiving—you can simply undo a mistaken step. It's like backing up to try again until you get it right.

So dive in. You'll be surprised at how much you can accomplish with just a little knowledge of the basics. If you like working with your hands, caning promises to give you hours of intense gratification.

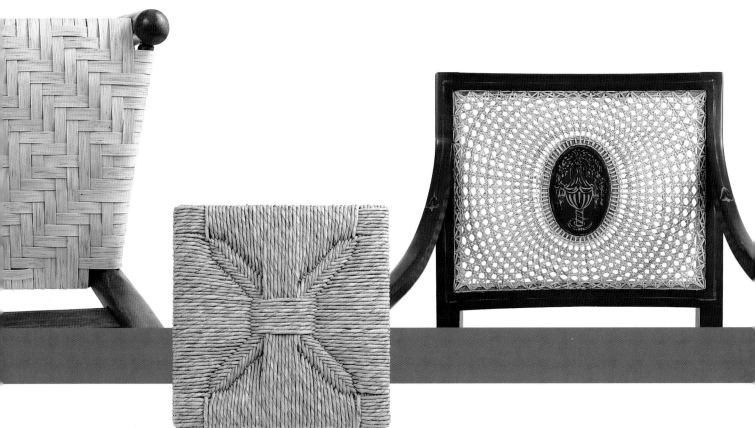

How to Find
Caning Tools and Materials

Most of the tools needed for re-caning furniture are common tools you probably have around your home or can find easily at your local hardware store.

There are a few specialized tools designed specifically to help professional caners work faster and more efficiently, but some of these are rare and difficult to find. This book shows you ways of making clever facsimiles of these specialty tools out of common household items. For example: a simple clothespin half becomes the perfect tool for one step in replacing a cane seat; a humble ice pick serves a multitude of purposes throughout the book. Who knows, you may come up with tools of your own.

Some communities have craft stores that carry an in-depth selection of tools and materials for all kinds of arts and crafts. Start by looking through the phone book to see what might be in your own backyard. Many of these stores carry pre-woven cane and various sizes of single-strand cane, as well as some types of splint and rush. You may be lucky enough to find one that is diverse enough to carry some of the specialty tools for hand caning furniture.

If there isn't a comprehensive craft store like this near you, try searching online. A general search can bring up a wide array of possible sources. Consider using broad search phrases like chair caning supplies, caning shops, wicker supplies, or rattan supplies to start.

When contacting stores and suppliers, you'll need to know exactly what to ask for. This book will help you learn how to do that, too.

Historical Highlights of Chair Caning Around the World

Seat weaving dates back thousands of years, as far back as the earliest civilizations. And yet, many characteristics of those early weaves and techniques still exist today.

When China opened its borders to foreign trade during the Ming Dynasty in 1567, many of the fine hardwood stools, chairs, and beds of the Chinese noble families were woven with finely cut cane using intricate twill patterns. Holes drilled through the frame held the individual strands of high quality cane imported from the Malay Peninsula.

The traditional octagonal pattern of cane was also woven on chair seats during the Ming Dynasty, the pattern having been derived from an earlier bamboo weaving technique. The edges of the caned frames were covered with another piece of hardwood and pegged into the holes to cover them and secure the cane.

A miniature Chinese bed

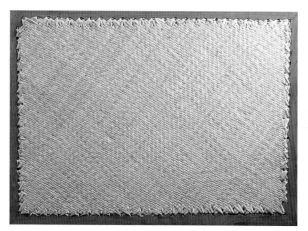

Example of close twill fabric woven onto the chair seat; the edges of the caned frame are then covered with a border of hardwood pegged into the holes.

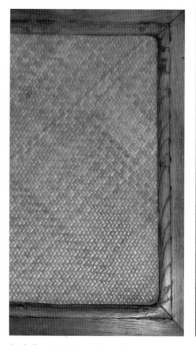

Left: Detail of the edge piece covering the drilled holes of a Ming Dynasty chair; courtesy of Red Lantern, Berkeley, California. *Right:* Detail of underside of Ming Dynasty seat; strong cordage is plaited first to give extra support for the woven seat.

From Ship Cables to Chair Seats

With the opening trade routes to the East Indies, the early Portuguese, Dutch, and English traders brought back spices, silks, and a new material—rattan—for making extremely strong cables for ships and ropes. They also brought the first examples of cane furniture to Europe, and by 1660, rattan and cane were making their first appearance as chair seats and backs. Europe imported whole rattan, but at first the cane was rustic and poorly cut. Within a few decades, however, willow basketmakers had learned to trim the cane into narrow, uniform lengths so that they could weave very fine and comfortable cane seats and backs for ornately carved wooden chairs.

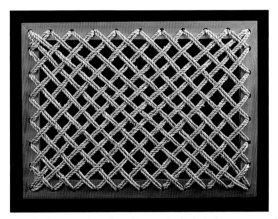

Detail of one ancient Egyptian method of plating a seat or bed with cordage made of rush through holes drilled into the frame

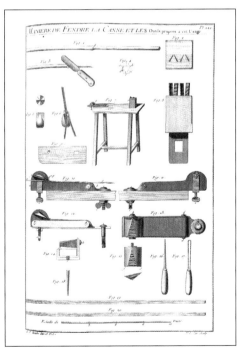

Tools for splitting and trimming rattan. Maniere de fender la canne et les outils Propres a cet usage. Roubo, André Jacob, *Description des arts et métiers*, Paris 1769-1775. Courtesy of The Winterthur Library: Printed Book and Periodical Collection

A Common Thread in Western History

Five thousand years ago, along the Nile, many of the chairs, stools, and beds used by the ruling families had a plaited pattern woven with cordage made from palm leaves, rushes, and leather thongs. The cordage passed through holes drilled into the framework. In some cases the plaiting was coarse and netlike, and in others the strands were tightly woven with little space in between.

For most of Western history, a chair as we know it was reserved for royalty and the very wealthy, yet even the wealthy owned only one or two chairs. When the Romans brought wicker to Europe in the fourth and fifth centuries, it was woven with willow and hedgerow and in the form of fencing, carriage bodies, storage trunks, and baskets. During the Middle Ages, craftsmen began producing chairs with splint seats of chestnut, ash, elm, or bulrush. Until the middle of the 17th century, common citizens still used stools and benches for all their seating needs.

Through the early seventeenth century, the American colonists continued the custom of reserving the seat of honor for guests while the host and hostess sat on benches and stools. The few chairs of this period were still made from turned wooden dowels or were stiff wooden chairs with wooden or stretched fabric seats.

The Basket Makers Guild in London and the Willow Weavers of France were well established by the time of the reign of Charles II, when a revolution in chair design occurred after the disastrous London Fire of 1666. The stiff architectural chair style that had prevailed was now supplanted by the graceful lines and carving of cane furniture, and there were plenty of skilled willow basket makers to weave the cane. The furniture style of turned and carved chairs with cane seats and backs were light and airy compared to the heavy wooden block chairs. A prosperous trade with England brought these new styles of furnishings to the New World.

In 1688, the woolen manufacturers in England petitioned the government to outlaw the manufacture of cane chairs. Upholsterers were facing wide-

Symonds collection, DAPC. Armchair, twist-turned frame, cane seat and back. England, c.1670. [59.35] Courtesy, The Winterthur Library

A Furniture Craze... 17th Century Style

"The introduction of chairs with cane bottoms and backs in northern Europe and America is one of the high points in the story of 17th century decorative arts as an international phenomenon. In no other form of furniture and at no other time do so many crosscurrents of political and commercial history and the history of taste come together to create so vividly a new style."

—Benno Forman, *American Seating Furniture: 1630–1730, An Interpretive Catalogue*

spread bankruptcy from the economic pressures of this new industry. More than 20,000 caned chairs were manufactured in London in that year alone.

With the burgeoning furniture trade with England, colonists saw the opportunity to make this new style of furniture themselves. *Chayremaker* as a profession, rather than turner or cabinetmaker, began showing up in the *Description of Trades* in the 1680s. With tools and machinery being simple and few, pursuing this new specialty was attractive to many.

The cane chair itself brought about a revolution in innovation. With its simplicity it could be mass-produced and thus be made affordable to a new class of consumers. Its simplicity allowed the chair maker to design new forms of chairs and break away from centuries-old forms. The cane chair introduced cane as a brand new type of upholstery material. For the next 150 years, the production of cane chairs continued through The Jacobean, Chippendale, Queen Anne, Banister Back, Windsor, and the Slat-back or Ladder-back chair styles.

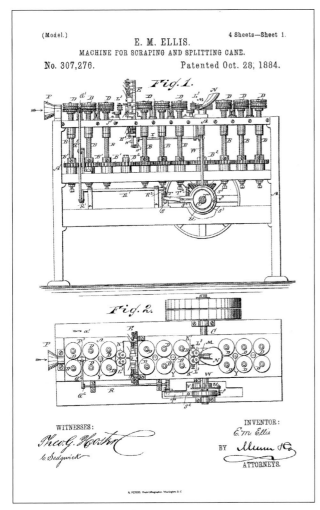

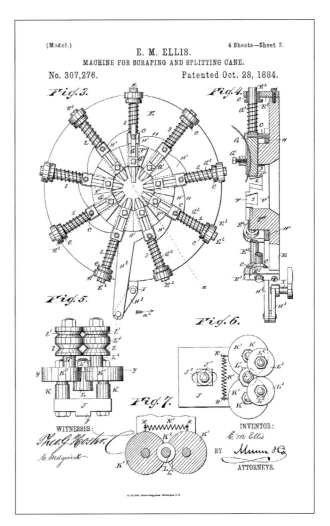

Patent drawings for machines to process rattan

A New American Industry

The tradition of designing a new, comfortable, lightweight chair continued in the United States in 1859 when Samuel Colt brought an entire village of German basketmakers to his arms factory along the Connecticut River to make willow furniture. At the same time, Michael Thonet and Sons in Vienna were developing a process for bending wood into forms that, when assembled, created beautiful flowing furniture. Thonet's inexpensive pieces were the beginning of the assemble yourself furniture trade. The woven cane seats were protected during shipment, and the parts needed only to be screwed together upon delivery.

Useful to the Core

At the same time, the American entrepreneur, Cyrus Wakefield, purchased rattan ballast from returning merchant ships and found that the material was ideally suited for creating bentwood designs without the laborious steaming process. In addition, the inner core, which is much more flexible than willow, could be easily coaxed into elaborate filigree work and airy woven patterns that were perfect for the sun porches and spacious verandas that adorned new summer homes and resorts around the country. During the early 1860s, Wakefield and Charles W. Trow invented new machines for polishing, splitting, and trimming rattan. These new procedures

Cottage workers splitting cane by hand, weaving cane mat: Photos courtesy of David Hall, Haas School of Business, University of California Berkeley, and the P3R Organization, Kalimantan, Indonesia

would spread across the United States, later to Germany, and finally back to Southeast Asia and China where the technology today is much the same as it was during Wakefield's day. Thus began a style of American furniture, which would influence furniture design around the world.

In Southeast Asia, rattan was a plentiful resource. While the peel was stripped from the rattan stalks for binding joints and weaving of mats, there was no need to further process the rattan core. If smaller diameter weaving material was necessary, there was another readily available length of whole rattan of the correct size. The core material was either burned for fuel or left to quickly rot and compost on the forest floor. No one had ever seriously considered using the unprotected core for weaving baskets and certainly not furniture. Without the protective peel, the inner core would quickly deteriorate, unlike bamboo or cane.

The Growing Industrial Revolution

In 1860, Samuel Colt's Willow Ware factory was setting the standard for graceful, almost rustic-style furniture. Thin willow branches could be split and shaved down to make thin strips of bark for wrapping joins. But willow was not nearly as forgiving a material to work as rattan. What Cyrus Wakefield

did with rattan, using the cane and splitting and dressing down the inner core to make intricate, filigree designs in furniture, was a transformation. The concurrent industrial revolution with its mechanization of so many tasks made Wakefield's technological breakthrough possible.

Until 1875, all of the cane fabric was handwoven strand by strand by women and children on farms around Gardner, Massachusetts, where Levi Heywood's company was located. The cottage cane fabric industry began declining in 1870 when Cyrus Wakefield and William Houston invented a loom to weave cane webbing for the seats of street cars and trolley cars.

Weaving in Mass Production

In the late 1870s, Gardner A. Watkins, working with Levi Heywood, revolutionized the cane seating industry by inventing an automatic channeling machine and an automatic crimping machine. With this new machinery, five people could quickly produce caned seat frames. The first worker created the channel in the seat frame; the second used a steel press to stamp out sections of webbing, then dampened the webbing with steam-heated water. The third used a hose and nozzle to fill the channel with a bead of glue; and the fourth aligned the sheet of

Evidence of Early Cane Weaving in Ancient China

In 1950, archaeologists returned to a tomb site in the Yellow River Valley first discovered in 1926. Among the ancient artifacts—brass and iron tools, coins, jade, gold, and horse-drawn carts—was a small fragment of weaving sandwiched between layers of sand. A very thin layer of fiber was carefully unearthed beneath a thin shard of brass. The pattern and actual material could be seen clearly. However the sand was so loose that when the section was moved the sand and the whole structure crumbled and the fiber was lost. Fortunately the basket had touched a piece of clay and left a trace on the clay. While the scientists referred to the pattern as bamboo, it likely was cane.

Facsimile of the clay fragment with cane impression found at Gu Wei Tomb #1, Shang Dynasty 1766-1050 BCE, Huixian County, Henan Province, China, in 1950

webbing over the seat space and then activated the machinery. The machine forced a brass crimping ring onto the webbing, pressing it into the groove. A fifth worker then used another machine to drive the triangular strip of wood into the groove, permanently anchoring the webbing in place. The entire process took just four minutes, including the initial machine weaving of the webbing.

Suddenly there was little need for a traditional caner, unless the customer preferred the traditional six-step open weave. But even this traditional pattern became mechanized and was in widespread use by 1879. However, the diagonal strands still had to be woven into the fabric by hand.

Again, a Hands-on Art

Today the caner is vitally necessary to restore the chair maker's legacy. Only the chair caner can reweave the hundreds of thousands of chairs made by the revolutionary craftsmen of the last 400 years. Whether it is a simple installation of pre-woven cane into a seat or back of a newer café chair or the intricate rebuilding and reweaving of a vintage Heywood-Wakefield wicker rocker, it is the chair-caner's skill and determination that will decide if the piece will last another 150 years or will disappear into the trash bin.

The Appeal and Ease of Using Pre-Woven Cane

Here's a basic technique that can help you reclaim that long-forgotten chair in your attic or restore a one-of-kind find at a secondhand store. If it's designed right, and the cane fixture can be replaced with a section of pre-woven cane webbing, this method opens up a world of possibilities. You'll quickly see the versatility and decorative flexibility of rattan.

AN EASY-TO-FIX PROBLEM:
REPLACING THE SEAT ON A CESCA SIDE CHAIR

Through the centuries, many furniture makers designed chairs in a way that allowed caners to re-cane the seats without significant obstacles. However, there have been several who designed chairs more specifically for easy assembly rather than easy seat replacement. Sometimes, the spline—or the wedge-shaped piece of reed used to hold the woven cane in place—was placed either directly under or too close to the chair back, or upholstery covered the spline. Other times, an arm brace or other chair parts completely covered the spline. If your chair fits this description, you may need to take it apart, or you may need a redesign of the seat attachment.

Fortunately, the Cesca Side Chair (opposite page), designed by Marcel Breuer, is easily re-caned without any preliminary reconstruction. The chair used in this example has a broken seat, a common problem that's easy to fix.

Machine cane, or cane webbing as it is called commercially, is manufactured from the outer bark or peel of the rattan palm. It is available in a variety of weaves ranging from the traditional octagonal pattern and close-woven basket weave to today's modern patterns.

Most cane webbing is available in widths up to 24 inches (61 cm), measured from selvage edge to selvage edge. Rolls of cane are available in continuous lengths up to 50 feet (15.2 m). Only the standard ½-inch (1.3 cm) cane webbing and the close-woven cane webbing are available in widths up to 36 inches (91.5 cm). The measurement of the cane pattern is based on the repetition of the pattern, not the hole in the pattern. The photographs illustrating the different cane webbing patterns found in Appendix A (page 117) are actual size. You can compare them to a swatch of webbing you're replacing to determine what size cane you'll need.

The Rattan Road Jungle Climber

Cane, the peel or bark from the rattan palm—or the entire stem in the case of the large-diameter, furniture-frame grade of rattan—grows throughout old world tropics from western Africa to Fiji, with the greatest abundance, diversity, and centers of origin in Southeast Asia. There are a few rattan species in Africa, but none are found in the Americas. While the family of rattan numbers over 600 species, only a few dozen of the species have the long internodes and strong, smooth bark necessary for the weaving of chair seats.

These rattans are found mostly in the tropical rain forests of Indonesia and Malaysia. Unlike other palms, rattan does not grow erect with a self-supporting trunk. The solid, uniform diameter canes wind their way to the top of the forest canopy by way of shoots that are covered with sharp hooks that grab onto the trunks of the rain forest trees.

PHOTO BY STEPHEN SEIBERT

Adjustable razor knife
⅛-inch (3 mm) chisel
Hooked-chisel
Dead-blow mallet or hammer
Flat chisel or putty knife
Rasp
Scissors
Clothespin half or bent ice pick
Pencil
Anvil rose pruner
White glue
Block of hardwood flooring

Ready for repair. This Cesca Side Chair, designed by Marcel Breuer, needs a new seat—an easy afternoon's work to reclaim a classic.

Removing the Old Seat

STEP 1

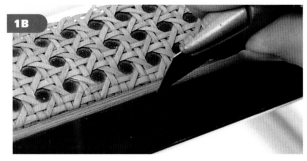

First, you'll need to use the adjustable razor knife to remove the major portion of the existing woven cane (photo 1A). Then you'll use the razor knife to begin separating the old cane from the spline (photo 1B). Carefully cut around the outside edge of the spline to separate the spline from the frame. Make several passes with the blade on each side of the spline (inside first, then outside), cutting a little deeper with each pass. Don't try to cut all the way to the bottom of the spline on the first or second pass. Each cut slowly separates the spline from the chair so as to minimize damage to the chair itself when removing the spline.

If you find the old spline particularly hard or stubborn, using a little water to soften it sometimes helps. Be sure to test the liquid on a hidden part of the finish first to avoid any potential damage. Using a small spray bottle, squirt a little water into your first cuts, letting it sit for a couple of hours to soften the glue.

STEP 2

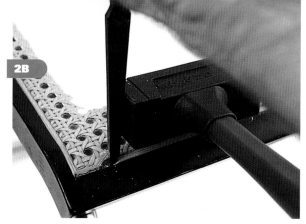

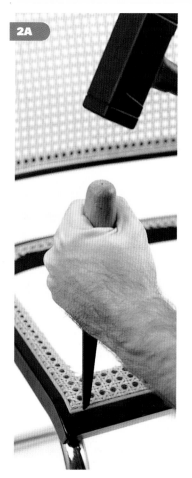

To remove the old spline, use the ⅛-inch (3 mm) mortise chisel or the hooked spline chisel. Hold the chisel vertically to the spline (photo 2A), and strike the end of the chisel once with the dead-blow mallet so that the chisel cuts deep into the spline. If you have one, a dead-blow mallet is easier to use than a regular steel hammer because its loaded end is designed to provide a consistent punch while minimizing potentially painful bounce back. Move the chisel 1 inch (2.5 cm) to the right, and with the chisel held vertically to the spline, again strike the end of the chisel once, making sure that the chisel cuts deeply into the spline.

After you make the second cut down into the spline, strike the chisel perpendicularly with the dead-blow mallet (photo 2B). (NOTE: This is **not** the proper way to use a chisel. Most chisels will break if used in this fashion. The ⅛-inch (3 mm) chisel shown in use here is a heavy-duty mortise chisel with a very thick shank. It's the only chisel I have found that can handle this type of abuse.) Striking the shank of the chisel horizontally shocks the short section of spline sideways, making it easier to remove.

Keep repeating this process of striking the chisel vertically, then the shank horizontally, around the perimeter of the seat. If the spline does not move immediately, don't worry, just keep moving the chisel to the right another inch and repeat the process. After several inches you will be rewarded with the spline sliding to the left, freeing it for easy removal.

The hooked spline chisel works using a similar method. Set the point of the hook against the spline and drive it into the spline with the dead-blow mallet with the handle of the chisel at

about the 10:00 position. Twist the handle of the chisel upward to about the 11:00 position and strike the edge of the curve of the chisel with the hammer to shock and move the section of spline to the left (photo 2C).

STEP 3

Now, it's time to thoroughly clean out the groove. Once the spline has been dislodged, hammer the chisel along the groove to clear out the spline. Cut away any remaining spline with the adjustable razor knife. Once the spline is removed, strip off any cane webbing still stuck to the groove.

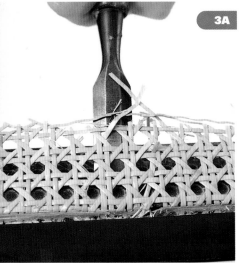

Use the flat chisel or putty knife to lift and remove the cane webbing that might be left glued to the chair seat. Carefully push it between the cane webbing and the wood of the chair seat, up to where the webbing goes into the groove (photos 3A, 3B). You merely want to detach the webbing, not cut it.

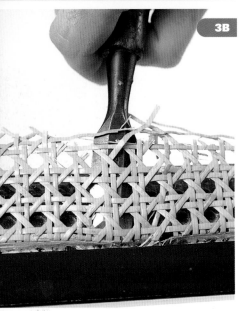

If you have difficulty separating the cane from the wood, spray a little water into the groove and let it sit for an hour or two to help dissolve the glue. Be careful with the water, though. It will soften the wood as well. Make sure all the cane, glue, and dust is removed from the groove before proceeding.

Replacing the Seat

STEP 1

Measure the size of the seat opening from groove to groove, front to back, then side to side, at the seat's widest points (photo 1A). To determine the measurements of the new cane webbing, add 2 inches (5 cm) to both measurements and round up to the next whole number.

Also, measure as accurately as possible the width of the groove to determine the size spline you'll need. You'll want to measure the width of the groove at various places around the seat to ensure the groove is a consistent width. If you cannot find the exact size spline you need, plane or dress down a wider piece with a small plane or sand gently with rough sandpaper.

STEP 2

Next, round any sharp inside edges of the seat frame with a rasp or rough sandpaper. Sharp edges will end up shortening the life of your new seat by cutting into the cane during use.

STEP 3

3A

Check the width of the spline you have chosen by putting it into the groove. If there is a space between the spline and the groove, the spline is too narrow. The sides of the spline should just brush the edges without needing to be forced into place (photo 3A). If the spline seems to be the correct width but protrudes well above the top of the groove, then the channel should be deepened to assure a comfortable fit for the cane. Be sure to maintain the vertical sides of the groove and a square edge at the bottom if you need to deepen it.

STEP 4

Soak the new woven cane in hot water for 15 minutes to ensure that it is pliable. Be careful not to soak the cane too long. Doing so will weaken it and cause the strands to turn a darker, greenish color. Also, you probably won't have to dampen the spline again later, unless you'll be forming it around a very tight bend.

STEP 5

5A

Center the new piece of cane over the seat and line up the strips with the edge of the seat (photo 5A), making sure that the double strands of cane are parallel to the front and back chair rails. There should be a strand of cane that runs along the chair rail just at the edge of the front and back grooves. Align the cane side to side so that one of the double strands lies along each side edge of the groove.

STEP 6

6A

The selvage edge of the cane (the side which has a string woven along the edge) should run along the front and back chair rails. Remove the string from the weave, making sure that the unraveled portion is beyond the visible finished chair seat and will not show. Remove the string from the selvage along the front edge of the seat. Notice that the chair's groove is in back of the string's location (photo 6A).

STEP 7

Unravel the strands that will lie outside the groove to lessen the chance of the cane breaking as it's being inserted. Using a thin wedge (without a sharp edge) or a wooden clothespin half, push the cane into the groove in just the middle of the front rail (photo 7A). Be careful not to cut the cane with the wedge. You want the cane to go all the way down into the groove and back up along the outside edge of the groove. If your wedge is too wide, the sides of the wedge will cut the cane before the wedge is all the way to the bottom of the groove. Tap in a small (1 inch [2.5 cm]) piece of spline to hold the cane in place (photo 7B).

Pull the cane to the back of the seat and push it into the middle of the back groove. Anchor it with a small piece of spline. Do the same for the other sides, after using the clothespin or wedge to push the cane into the groove. The cane should be held in place at four points.

STEP 8

Trim the back corners of the cane so that the rounded edge is 1 inch larger than the caned area (photo 8A). Remove or unravel the cane along and

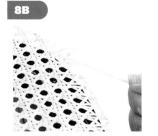

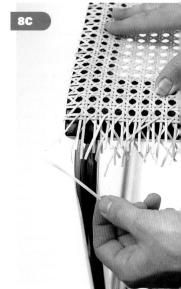

up to the side rails so that you'll be able to push the cane into the groove without breaking it (photo 8B). Remove any extra diagonal strands along the front corners (photo 8C).

STEP 9

Start pushing the cane into the groove, working from the middle of the rail out to the corner. You can use the wooden clothespin half for this task (photo 9A), or an ice pick that has been bent into a right-angle (photo 9B). To ensure even tension in the weave, always start in the middle of

the rail next to the anchor and work toward the corner, working the two sides first, then the front and back rails.

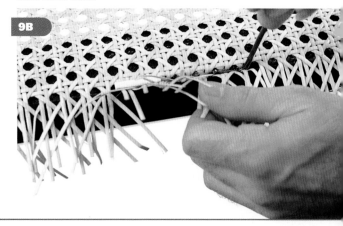

STEP 10

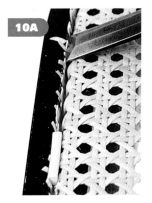

After all the cane has been set into the groove, trim the cane with the flat chisel or the utility knife just below the outside edge of the groove (photos 10A, 10B). Remove the remaining anchors from the sides and back of the seat.

Setting the Spline

STEP 1

Start setting the spline into the right front corner (as you face the chair). Lay the spline on top of the corner and mark the angle of the miter join with a pencil (photo 1A). Using the rose pruners or sharp garden shears, undercut the mark made with the pencil (photo 1B). The shears should cut through the pencil line, leaving the section below the top of the spline very slightly undercut.

STEP 2

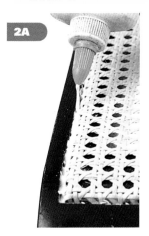

Pour a generous amount of white glue into the groove on top of the cane (photo 2A). Don't be timid. If you use too much glue it will clean up easily with water when you are finished. If you put in too little glue, the spline will pop out when the chair is used.

STEP 3

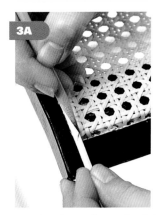

Carefully align the cut end of the spline into the corner with the mallet, making sure that the join is seated properly in the corner. Set in the rest of the length of spline, tapered end down, around the back of the chair seat almost to the left-hand corner. Mark where the end of the spline will be on the left-hand corner of the seat (photo 3A). Carefully undercut this miter join and tap the end of the spline into the corner.

STEP 4

After tapping the spline into the groove with the hammer, use a block of hardwood flooring to set the spline flush with the top of the groove (photo 4A).

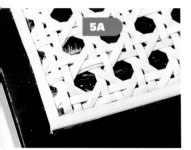
5A

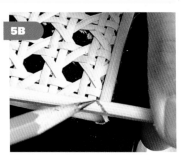
5B

Using a new section of spline, measure and under-cut the corners of the spline for the front rail. Make sure the angles match and the length is correct (photo 5A). After tapping the spline into the front rail, go back and trim the corners so that they make a perfect match (photo 5B). Use the hardwood flooring block to tap the front spline into a flush position.

The Caner's Corner

Dealing with Different Shaped Seats

If your chair has a continuous groove without corners, such as a round bentwood chair seat, begin in the center of the back groove. If there are sharp corners, you'll have to set the spline in sections. Miter the corners. Tap the spline down until it is flush with the frame.

Finishing Touches

After the cane has dried overnight, it can be colored with a varnish or lacquer stain or left natural to tan with age. Cane (rattan peel) needs to breathe. It can only absorb moisture and oils from the underside. The shiny bark contains a lot of silica and acts as a moisture barrier. I recommend aerosol finishes since they can be applied to the surface of the cane. Stains and finishes that are brushed on or wiped on tend to flow around to the underside of the cane, sealing the material. If cane can't breathe and absorb moisture and oils, it becomes dried out, brittle, and prone to damage.

Taking Care of Your New Cane Seat

Natural chair cane has a memory, and after a new seat is first used the cane will naturally tighten up when the pressure is taken off. As the chair is used over time, the cane begins to lose its memory and stretch or sag. The danger at this point is that when the chair is used, the cane will begin to wear against the edges of the chair and break. Restore the tension in the cane by wetting it with hot water, and let it dry. This will shrink it naturally.

First, turn the chair over on a towel. Wet the cane with hot water and a sponge on the underside of the cane where it will absorb the moisture. Be careful not to get the wood wet. Immediately turn the chair over and wipe off any moisture on the wood and place a wet towel on top of the cane for about 30 minutes. Put the chair in a corner where no one will sit on it for 24 hours, and let it dry naturally. The cane should tighten up as good as new.

After a number of years, the cane will begin to dry out. A light coat of lemon oil on the underside of the cane will help keep the cane from becoming brittle. Be sure to wipe off any excess oil after five minutes. Remember, cane is a natural material that should be protected from conditions that will cause it to dry out and become brittle. Direct sunlight and heater ducts are areas to be avoided.

Refined and ready. The completed Cesca Side Chair

The Rattan Road Weaving Strands of Trade

Cane used in weaving large rolls of cane webbing undergoes additional processes to prepare it for use in the looms. Since the looms produce rolls of cane up to 50 feet (15.25 m) in length, the warp strands of cane—the strands that run the full length of the roll—must be joined together to make a continuous strand of cane more than 50 feet (15.25 m) long. Factory workers scrape the top of the end of one strand and the bottom of the joining strand and glue them together to make an adequately long strand.

As the strand grows in length, it is rolled onto a large bobbin which will be mounted on the loom. A roll of cane 12 inches (30.5 cm) wide will require a minimum of 48 bobbins of chair cane for the warping of the loom. The cane loom is similar to a harness loom for weaving fabric. The long cane strands, spooled onto bobbins, form the warp strands. The loom operator feeds the weavers one by one into the weave.

Since no loom can weave a diagonal strand, the diagonals must be woven in one by one after the basic grid is loomed. Afterward, the rolls of cane are checked for small breaks or missing strands and repaired. The woven rolls of cane are put through a bleach bath to insure that the color is uniform throughout the roll. Then the woven mesh is dried, ironed flat, and spooled into a tight 50-foot (15.2 m) roll.

Above, left: Loom for weaving cane fabric. *Above, center:* Workers weaving open cane fabric. *Above, right:* Weaving the diagonal strands into open fabric. PHOTOS BY CHRIS CHAN. *Left:* Ironing the cane fabric and rolling it into rolls for shipping. Above: checking the cane fabric and repairing defects in the weave. PHOTOS BY DENNIS LEE

OTHER CREATIVE AND DECORATIVE USES FOR MACHINE CANE

Pre-woven cane is incredibly versatile. The modern look of natural cane blends well with cabinetry in the home and can lend a decorative helping hand in countless other circumstances. It's available in traditional and modern weaves of natural cane and a cane look-alike made from resin impregnated paper. While natural cane can be used in most cases, the paper-based fiber and some of the modern, more open weaves made from natural cane should be used in a more ornamental sense, and not for seats of furniture. The strands are simply not strong enough to handle the use.

Since woven cane is open and airy, it helps with ventilation. As a result, many yacht owners have found it to be perfect for galley and storage cabinet doors.

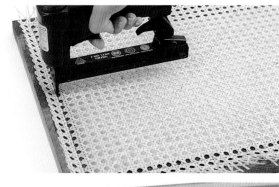

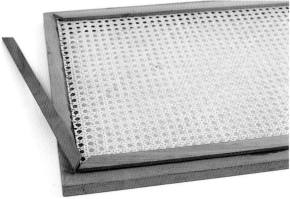

Above, top: Stapling cane fabric to a frame. *Above:* Wood stops added to cover the stapled edge of cane fabric

There are four primary methods of applying cane webbing to wood framework. They range from extremely easy to very intricate:
• The cane is held in place with a piece of spline inserted into a groove in the top of the wood frame.
• Using a groove and spline (or staples), but applying the cane on the underside (or backside) of the wood frame (below left, top), with the shiny side of the cane facing through the hole in the panel. The staple heads are hidden by strips of wood or rattan.
• Constructing an inner frame upon which the cane is attached, either stapled or with a spline, that fits into the wood frame (below left, bottom).
• Gluing the cane to a plywood panel which is then inserted into the wood frame.

Another alternative is to drill holes through the panel and then hand cane the panel rather than use pre-woven cane. This technique is discussed in detail in the next chapter.

For all the following methods, you must remember in your design, that as cane webbing dries it exerts a tremendous amount of pressure and will distort or bend the framework if the wooden members are too thin or too long. On a tall door, either plan to make two or three panels, depending on the height of the door, or put in one or two stretcher bars to keep the sides parallel.

Below: Finished side up. Two examples of finished cane fabric speaker covers

CABINET DOORS, SPEAKER FRONTS, GALLEY VENTILATION

STEP 1

Soak the cane in hot water for five to 10 minutes. Shake out the excess water. Align the wet sheet of cane so that the good (front) side is facing the front of the door. Make sure the cane is aligned horizontally and vertically to the door frame.

STEP 2

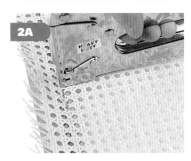

Use a T-50 stapler or an upholsterers pneumatic stapler to drive the staples into the lip of the door frame. As with the chair seat, start in the middle of the rail and work toward the corners (photo 2A). Staple every pair of strands.

Trim the cane with the adjustable razor knife (photo 2B).

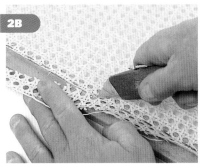

Finished galley door from the Catena, owned by Ed Ferranto

Finishes for Cabinet Doors

Since cane webbing in cabinet doors usually won't get any pressure, it's not as critical to avoid finishes that make the cane brittle. However, I would still recommend using an aerosol application to only the front side of the cane if a color is necessary. The best approach would be to leave the cane in its natural state and allow the gradual darkening through age. As with other cane furniture, an occasional light application of furniture or lemon oil to the back side of the cane will help lengthen the life of your work. (Make sure to wipe up any excess immediately after the application.)

Cabinet doors on boats offer a different set of challenges. The high humidity found on boats will cause the cane webbing to always be in a saggy state, no matter how taut the cane was stretched when it was initially applied. Unless the door panels are very small, where the sagging cane will not be so noticeable, a finish that seals the cane is more desirable. Another solution might be to use one of the patterns of the alternative paper-based cane. These will not be susceptible to changes in humidity.

USING RAFFIA CLOTH, PRE-WOVEN CANE, OR SEAGRASS MATTING AS DECORATIVE COVERING

Another versatile use of pre-woven cane is that it can serve as a decorative covering for tables, trays, or other flat surfaces. It's a perfect way to add a texture to a surface that needs a little extra emphasis. In this example, the focus is on a small bamboo table that had been covered once before, but needs to be recovered due to wear and tear.

Tools and Materials

Hobby knife or adjustable razor knife
Sandpaper
Clear contact cement
2-inch (5 cm) paintbrush
Acetone or lacquer thinner
Raffia cloth, pre-woven cane webbing or
    seagrass matting (a.k.a. Chinese Beach Mat)
2-inch (5 cm) paint roller
½-inch (1.3 cm) x 20-gauge brads
Tack hammer

STEP 1

1A

In our example, there are four pieces of split rattan anchoring the edge of the old mat that must be removed. Many tables and trays have similar features. In situations like this, it's better to pry up the whole piece slowly rather than trying to lift one end completely before removing the next nail.

Remove the old matting and scrape away as much of the old glue as possible. Sand the top as smooth as possible. Clean away all the dust (photo 1A).

STEP 2

2A

Use a quality, *clear* contact cement. Apply the contact cement to the tabletop with a wide brush in a very well-ventilated area, making sure you completely cover the entire top (photo 2A). Follow the manufacturer's directions. Be careful not to get any cement on the other parts of the table. If you do, you can remove it with nail polish remover or lacquer thinner.

Apply a coat of contact cement to the raffia cloth (or cane fabric or seagrass matting), making sure you cover an area equal to or larger than the tabletop (photo 2B). Let the contact cement dry for as long of a period as the manufacturer recommends—usually 10 minutes.

STEP 3

Start at one end of the tabletop and carefully set the fabric, cement side down, on the tabletop in exactly the position you want it. (Be careful—once the two cemented surfaces touch, they will not release.) Carefully roll the matting out so that it is aligned with the tabletop (photo 3A).

Use a short paint roller to bond the two surfaces together and to remove any bubbles that might have formed (photo 3B). Trim the matting at the tabletop edge with a sharp hobby knife blade.

Set the split rattan pieces in place, and nail them to the edge of the table so that they cover the edge of the matting. Use ½-inch (1.3 cm), 20-gauge brads (photo 3C).

Top this. The finished table with newly refinished top.

Gallery

Wing back rocker with medallion set into center back panel

Side chair with ½-inch (2.3 cm) woven cane set into the seat and rattan curlicues set into back with rattan wraps to hold the back into position

Barrel back chair open weave set into the seat and the back

Dining chair with radio net weave set
into the seat and the back

Vanity stool with
woven cane set into
the seat and on both sides
(double caned) of the back rest

High chair with close-woven cane set
into the seat and the back

Mending Classics:
Time-Honored Hand Caning Techniques

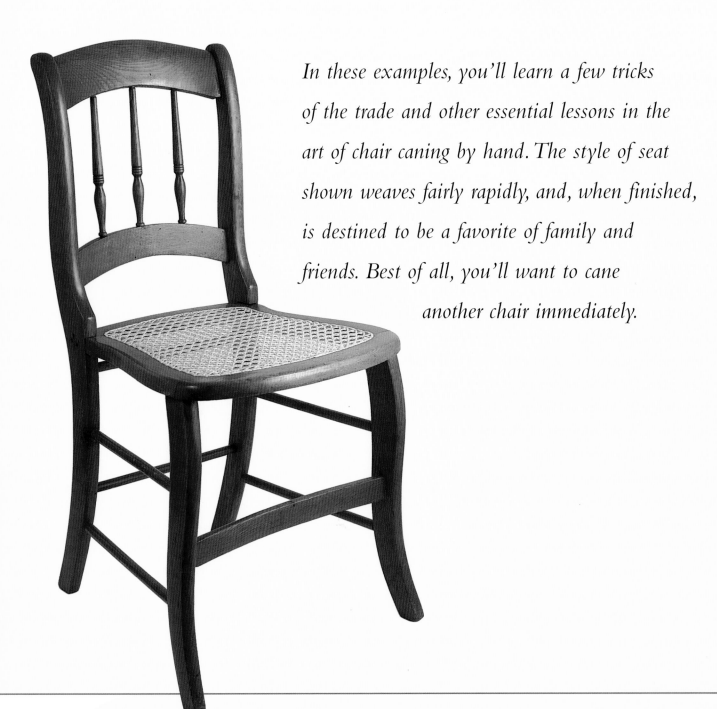

In these examples, you'll learn a few tricks of the trade and other essential lessons in the art of chair caning by hand. The style of seat shown weaves fairly rapidly, and, when finished, is destined to be a favorite of family and friends. Best of all, you'll want to cane another chair immediately.

HAND CANING AN 1870s' FACTORY-MADE MAPLE CHAIR

Getting Started

If you're new to chair caning, you should probably look for a chair that has no more than 72 holes drilled around the edge and with a spacing of at least ½-inch (1.3 cm) between the holes (when measured from the center of one hole to the center of the next hole). Also, look for a chair with a caned area that is square, rectangular, or trapezoid shape. A slightly rounded front rail is OK. Steer clear of round seats until you have gained a little more experience. The chair shown in this project (opposite page) offers a terrific shape for any skill level.

This chair also illustrates a common injury—the seat rail has a split running through the holes around the seat rail (left). Notice also that the cane has torn along the front seat rail (below). Coincidentally, the tear is right above the sharp inner edge of the front rail. As a cane seat ages, it begins to sag and rub against the inner edge of the seat rail. If the rail edge is sharp, you can imagine the outcome. Luckily you can fix this problem and restore a fabulous antique to its former glory.

Tools and Materials

Tape measure
Pencil
Hobby knife
Caning awl (or a long, slender ice pick)
Rasp, coarse sandpaper, or plane
Sharp scissors
Caning pegs (24 minimum)
Sponge
Container of hot water
Wire loop tool
Clothespins for bundling single lengths
   of cane for soaking
Chair cane

*You may also need the following
   for chair repairs:*
White glue or woodworking glue
Counter sink/pilot bit (to fit #8 x 1½ inch
   [3.8 cm] screws)
Panel screws: #8 x 1½ inches (3.8 cm)
Power drill
Wood putty
Furniture clamps
C-clamps

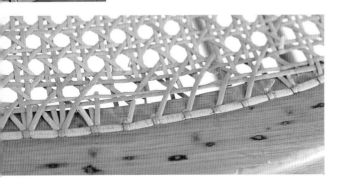

The Caner's Corner

Determining What Size Cane to Use

The spacing of the holes drilled in the framework of the chair determines what size cane is needed and the pattern to be woven. Measure the spacing of the holes along the side rail of the chair. Measure from the center of one hole to the center of the next.

Sometimes, the holes are not always drilled exactly the same distance between each hole and can be off by as much as ¼ inch (6 mm). This can throw off your calculations. I've developed a system that will help you figure out what you need, and it's based on how many holes there are in a 6-inch (15.2 cm) measurement of the rail.

First, lay the ruler at the beginning of one hole along the side rail so that the first hole is completely within the measurement (photo at right). Count the number of holes in 6 inches. If the last hole is partly included

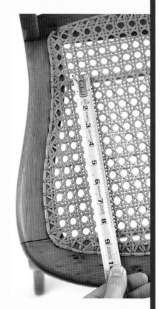

within the 6 inches, count it. If the last hole is just beyond 6 inches, don't count it. Use the chart below to determine the cane size to use for reweaving the seat.

I prefer measuring along the side rails rather than the back or front rails. Over the years, I have found the side rails to be a more consistent indicator. For this project, there are 10 holes, so the size of cane to use is Narrow Medium.

Number of holes in 6 inches	Spacing between the holes (center to center)	Size of Cane
8	⅞ inch	Common 3.5 mm
9	¾ inch	Medium 3.0 mm
10	¹¹⁄₁₆ inch	Narrow Medium 2.75 mm
11	⅝ inch	Fine 2.5 mm
12	½ inch	Fine-Fine 2.25 mm
13	⁷⁄₁₆ inch	Super Fine 2.0 mm
14	⅜ inch	Carriage Fine 1.75 mm
16	¼ inch	Carriage Super Fine 1.50 mm

Preparing Your Chair for Re-Caning

STEP 1

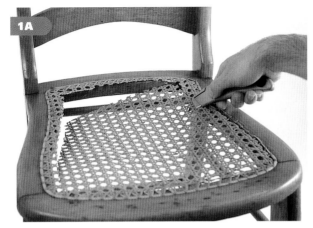

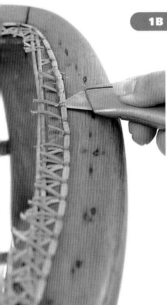

If the frame of your chair needs repairs—like re-gluing or refinishing—take care of them before trying to reweave the chair.

First, you'll need to remove the old cane and inspect the seat thoroughly. Start by cutting out the main section of cane close to the edge of the chair seat frame (photo 1A). Use an adjustable razor knife or hobby knife to carefully cut the cane loops holding the binder cane in place (photo 1B).

Remove the binder cane and then use the caning awl (or a long, slender ice pick) to unravel any cane still woven to the chair seat. Turn the chair over and use the awl or pick to loosen the loops of cane underneath the chair seat. Be careful not to scratch the finish of the wood with the sharp tip. Make sure the holes are all clear and all the cane and dust have been removed.

To repair a split seat rail, you'll need to carefully glue the split back together using a woodworking glue or white glue and several clamps. Make sure

the wood grain lines up and all of the loose wood pieces are in the correct places. Use a counter sink/pilot bit for a #8 x 1½ inch (3.8 cm) wood screw and drill three to five pilot holes, spread out over the length of the seat rail (photo 1C). Make sure none of the pilot holes pass through the holes that will be used for caning. Do not drill a pilot hole within the first inch (2.5 cm) at either end of the seat rail. This might split the wood yet again.

After drilling and countersinking the pilot holes through the repaired split in the seat rail, carefully screw #8 x 1½-inch (3.8 cm) panel screws into the seat rail to secure the glued repair. (Panel screws have coarser threads than wood screws and tend to hold better than wood screws.) Use wood putty to fill any missing sections of wood between the holes on top and underneath the seat rail. If any wood putty sticks in the hole, drill it out before continuing.

If the chair joins are loose, this is a good time to re-glue the chair. Use good woodworking glue and furniture clamps to make sure all of the joins of the chair and seat frame are tight. A wobbly chair is not worth caning. It will likely fail and could prove to be a safety hazard for those who use it.

As you recall, the sharp edge of the seat rail cut the cane. To get rid of the edge, use the rasp, coarse sandpaper, or a plane to soften this sharp edge (photo 1D).

"In general, cane chairs became fashionable in France only about 25 or 30 years ago [ca. 1740]. They are very serviceable, and much neater than straw—or rush-bottom chairs, whether the frames of these latter are made by joiners—very rare at present—or by turner—almost the only ones who make such chairs for the common folk or for inconsequential rooms."

—André Jacob Roubo, 1762, translated by Benno M. Forman, *American Seating Furniture, 1630-1730: An Interpretive Catalogue*

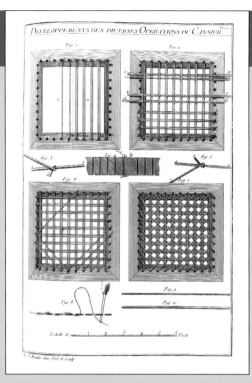

Courtesy of The Winterthur Library: Printed Book and Periodical Collection

Advertisement for platform rockers by the Wakefield Rattan Company

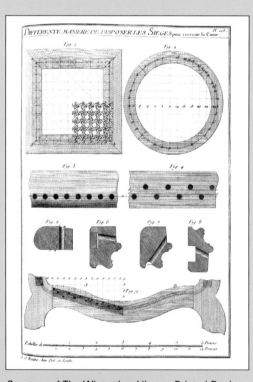

Courtesy of The Winterthur Library: Printed Book and Periodical Collection

Weaving The First Course

STEP 1

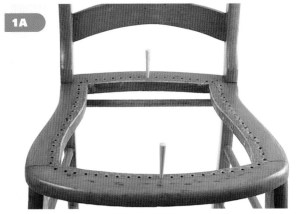

Determine the center hole on the front and back seat rails. If there's an odd number of holes, then the center hole will be easy to determine. If the number is even, choose the hole just to the right of the center of both the front and back rails. It's important that you be consistent in your choice or the first course will not be square to the chair. Put a caning peg into the center hole in the back rail and the center hole of the front rail (photo 1A).

STEP 2

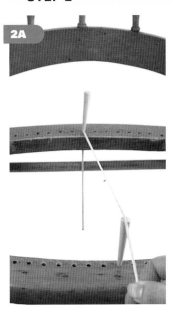

Insert 6 inches (15.2 cm) of cane into the pegged hole (remove the peg, insert the cane, and re-insert the peg into the hole to secure the cane) in the back rail. Bring the cane forward to the pegged hole in the front rail (photo 2A). Always keep the glossy bark of the cane up so that it always shows.

STEP 3

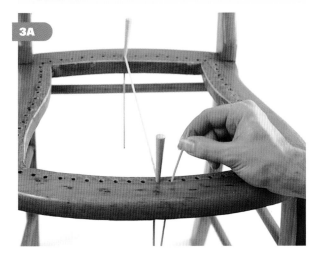

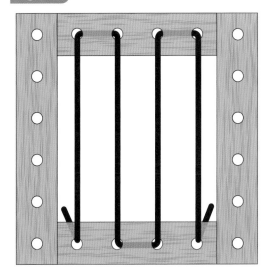

Figure 1

Remove the front peg, pull the cane snug, insert it into the hole, then replace the peg to secure the cane (photo 3A). Bring the end up through the adjacent hole to the right of the pegged hole (figure 1). Pull the cane snug. Make sure there is no twist in the loop on the underside of the seat, and move the peg in the front rail to secure the cane. Again, make sure the glossy bark of the cane is showing on the loop as well as the seat.

STEP 4

Continue pulling the cane snug, passing it from top to bottom through the adjacent holes, making sure the loops on the underside of the seat have no twists. Advance the peg to continue securing the cane in the most recent hole (photo 4A). Make sure that the cane remains snug. There should be no slack in the weave.

STEP 5

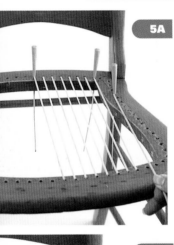

If your chair is like the one in this example, weave only diagonal strands into the corner holes. The last vertical (front to back) strand will be one hole short of the corner. The next row is a *short* row since it will not be as long as the row immediately to its left. Peg a new strand of cane into a hole in the side rail so that the strand will still be parallel to the previous rows (photo 5A). Bring the strand to the front rail and insert it into the next hole to the right of the last row.

Insert the strand into the hole and bring it out of the adjacent hole to the right. This chair has room for two short rows on either side of the seat, so pass the strand to another hole on the side rail such that the vertical (back to front) rows are parallel and evenly spaced (photo 5B). Peg the strand into the hole, keeping the strands snug.

STEP 6

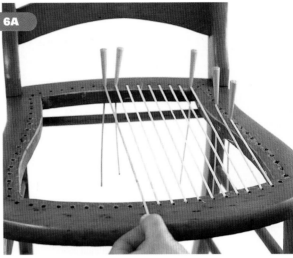

One half of the first course is now complete. Peg a new strand into the back rail in the hole that is just to the left of the starting hole for the first course (photo 6A). Pull the strand snug toward the front rail and insert it into the first free hole in the front of the chair rail. Secure it with a new peg and bring the strand up through the hole that is to the left of this hole . Keep the strands snug, and watch for twists in the loops underneath the seat rail.

Now, finish the first course in the same manner as before and weave in two short rows on the left side of the seat, making sure that all the rows are parallel (photo 6B).

Weaving the Second Course

The second course does not weave, but lies on top of the first course.

STEP 1

Begin the second course by either pegging a new strand into the middle of the left chair seat rail, or by bringing the remainder of the strand from the short row from the first course up the adjacent hole and over to the opposite side rail. Determine the equivalent hole on the opposite side (photo 1A) by counting the holes on both sides to make sure that the holes are truly opposite one another.

STEP 2

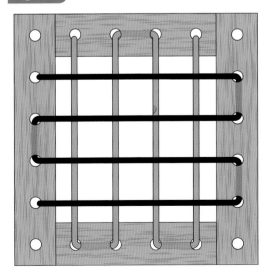

Do not weave this strand. Bring it across, on top of the first course, and insert the strand into the

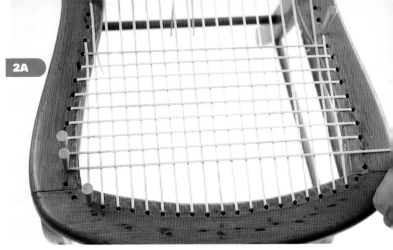

appropriate hole (figure 2). Peg the strand to secure it, bring the strand up through the adjacent hole and back across to the opposite side as you did in the first course (photo 2A).

If you run out of cane in the middle of a step, simply peg and start a new piece to finish the step.

STEP 3

Remember to keep the corner hole reserved for the diagonal strands. Skip the corner hole and put in one last short row across the front of the seat. Finish the second course by continuing to weave the strands from side to side to fill in the back half of the seat (photo 3A).

The chair in this example needs one short row along the back edge as well. Skip the corner hole and draw the cane through the hole that is adjacent to the corner hole along the back rail (photo 3B).

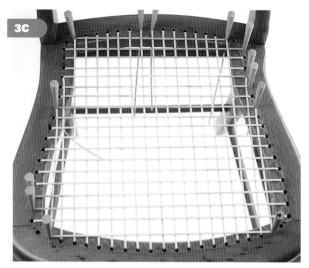

The second course is now complete, including the short row along the back (photo 3C).

STEP 4

It is a good habit to tie off loose strands as soon as there is a loop of cane adjacent to the strand. First, dampen the loops as well as the cane that is hanging from the seat with a sponge and hot water. After dampening, slightly lift the loop with the tip of the caning awl so that the tip of the cane can pass under the loop (photo 4A). Be careful not to lift the loop too high or it will snap. Pass the cane under the loop as far as you can and pull snug.

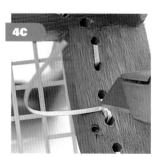

Then tuck the end of the strand under the loop a second time and pull snug (photo 4B).

Trim the end of the strand flush with the loop to hide the end (photo 4C).

Weaving the Third Course

The third course does not weave but lies on top of the first and second courses.

STEP 1

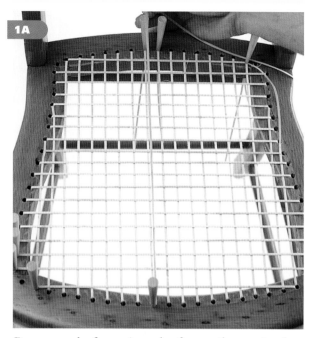

Peg a strand of cane into the front rail opposite the left-hand peg in the back rail (photo 1A). The strands for the third course will go into the same holes as the strands from the first course, but they will be slightly to the right of the strands from the

Figure 3

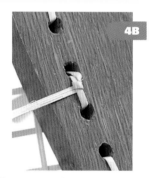

first course (figure 3). Fill in the section on the left-hand side of the chair. Inspect the underside of the

seat to make sure the loops are filling the space between the loops of the first course and not doubling on top of them. Make sure the strand of the third course is to the right of the strand of the first course (photo 1B).

STEP 2

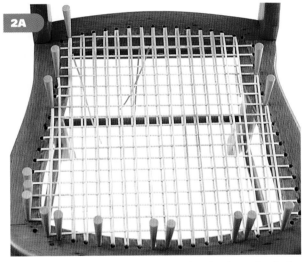

After the third course has been finished on the left-hand side of the chair, peg a new strand of cane into the adjacent hole on the front rail, and slightly to the right of the first course below it. Finish stringing the third course until the right half of the

seat is completed (photo 2A). Again, inspect the underside of the chair seat after finishing the third course and tying off any loose strands. Make sure the loops are evenly spaced all around the seat frame.

Weaving the Fourth Course

This is actually the first weaving step.

STEP 1

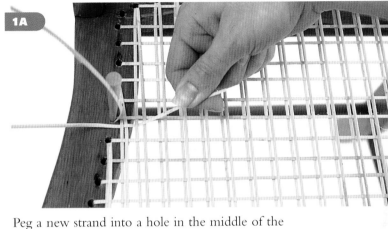

Peg a new strand into a hole in the middle of the left side rail. The fourth course is woven to the front of the second course—woven between you and the strand from the second course that occupies the same hole that you are now using (photo 1A). The strand will weave under the strand from the first course and over the strand from the third course, then under the strand from the first course

---

The Caner's Corner

Going in the Right Direction

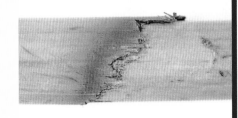

There is a *high* side and a *low* side of the leaf node (right). The end of the strand on the *low* side should be pegged into the chair. Always weave so that the *high* side of the leaf node passes through the weave first.

You can feel the high side of the node by running your fingernail against it. In one direction your nail will *catch*. The strands of cane in the weave will also *catch* and strip or fray the cane. When the *high* side of the node goes through the weave first, the strand pulls through smoothly without catching.

Figure 4

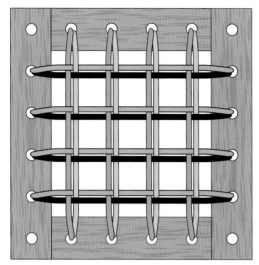

and over the strand from the third course until you have woven approximately ⅓ of the way across the seat (figure 4).

STEP 2

2A

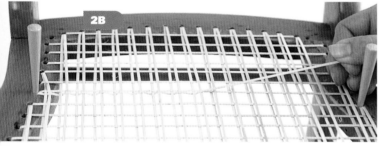

2B

When you have woven one-third the distance across the seat, pull all of the excess cane through the weave, being careful to avoid any twists in the cane and keeping the glossy bark to the top (photos 2A, 2B). In the photo 2B, notice that all of the excess cane has been pulled through the weave and that this strand appears to go up and down while

the three other strands from the previous courses are straight. Give the strand an additional tug. This will cause the up-and-down appearance to disappear as the other strands in the weave take up the tension of the new strand. Continue weaving across the seat to the opposite hole, one-third the total distance at a time. Be sure to pull the slack and give an extra tug before continuing.

STEP 3

3A

Use the tip of the caning awl to slightly lift the vertical (back to front) strand that is on top of the wood of the seat so that the horizontal (side-to-side) strand of the fourth course can weave the last intersection before going into the hole (photo 3A). Be sure to give the strand an additional tug to even out the tension before passing the strand into the hole and up through the next hole.

Inspect where you are at this point. Notice that some of the strands have been paired while others have not. The grid is not uniform. Some of the strands are wobbly. This will be fixed in the next step.

STEP 4

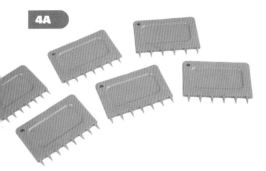
4A

4B

French caners invented a set of combs for straightening the weave while hand caning. Each comb is made for a particular pattern spacing (photo 4A). The tapered teeth of the comb just fit in the larger spaces of the weave between the pairs of strands when the grid is exactly perfect (photo 4B). Use the comb to move or push the pairs of strands into position.

If you don't have access to caning combs, the tack hammer and the caning awl can be used to straighten the grid by moving one small section of cane at a time (photo 4C). Also, two caning pegs held at opposite sides of the intersection of the four strands of cane can be used to push the individual strands of cane into position.

4C

The Caner's Corner

Leftover Strands: An Alternative Method

Here's another way to take care of the leftover strands of cane besides tying them off on the bottom.

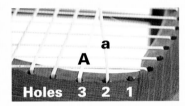
Holes 3 2 1

Strand end *a* is the end of strand *A* brought up through the adjacent hole number two, but not long enough to go to the opposite side of the chair.

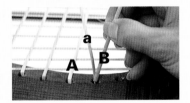

Strand *B* is the new strand inserted into hole number two and in front of *a* in the hole.

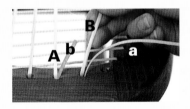

End *b* is the end of strand *B* brought up through hole number three and behind strand *A* so that when a is pulled snug, it locks *b* into place.

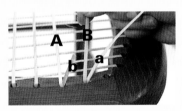

Position *B* in front of *a*, pull snug, and then take *B* to the hole on the opposite side, continuing the weaving pattern.

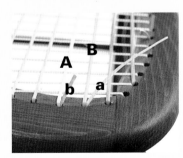

The splice is complete. The old strand *A* and the new strand *B* have locked each other into position. No tying off on the underside is necessary. Loops from successive courses will also help lock the strands into position.

The Rattan Road
Hand Caning in a Mechanized Age

As early as the late 17th century, skilled European craftsmen were weaving chair seats with an octagonal pattern using cane brought to Europe from Southeast Asia by English traders. Not only were they weaving the cane, they were preparing chair cane from imported whole rattan vines. These early caners were probably willow basketmakers, used to skeining and weaving willows and rushes into baskets, trunks, and carriage bodies.

By 1680, caned chairs imported from England were showing up in the American colonies, and by 1700, American chairmakers were importing the materials and caning the chairs themselves. For the next 150 years, all caned chairs made in the American Colonies were hand caned with materials split, trimmed, and sized by the caner. Sullivan Sawyer of Massachusetts invented machines for cutting, splitting, and dressing rattan in 1849. This made it possible for the hundreds of thousands of chairs being manufactured domestically to be caned in a timely manner. Chair caning became a cottage industry for whole neighborhoods that surrounded chair-making factories.

To meet the growing demand for cane fabric, a loom for weaving close-woven cane webbing was invented in 1867 by Gardner Watkins, and by 1881, even the open, traditional octagonal pattern had become mechanized.

Shortly thereafter, the stitched binder, an extra step meant to provide a finished edge to the handcaned seat, began to see widespread use. It could be that the wooden spline—encircling the pre-woven cane seats—inspired this crowning step. Up to then, the only attempt to hide the holes drilled in chair frames had been by the Chinese with 1-inch-wide (2.5 cm) pieces of wood that were pegged into the holes and covered each edge of the seat frame.

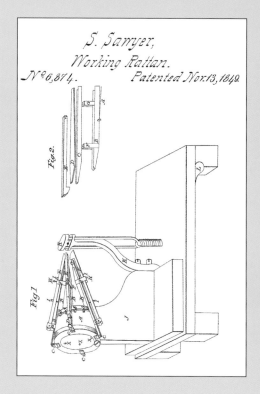

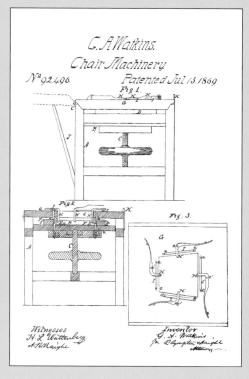

Patents for cane working machinery by Sullivan Sawyer and Gardner Watkins

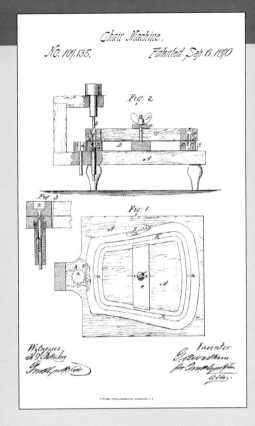

Chair Machine,
No. 107,135.   Patented Sep. 6. 1870.

Fig. 2.

Fig. 3   Fig. 1.

Witnesses   Inventor

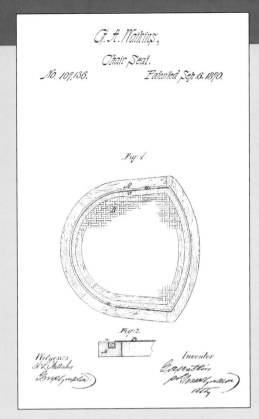

G. A. Watkins,
Chair Seat.
No. 107,136.   Patented Sep. 6. 1870.

Fig. 1.

Fig. 2.

Witnesses   Inventor

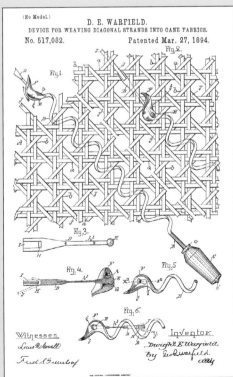

(No Model.)
D. E. WARFIELD.
DEVICE FOR WEAVING DIAGONAL STRANDS INTO CANE FABRICS.
No. 517,082.   Patented Mar. 27, 1894.

Fig. 2.
Fig. 1.
Fig. 3.
Fig. 4.   Fig. 5.
Fig. 6.

Witnesses   Inventor
Dwight E. Warfield.
By Geo. Warfield atty.

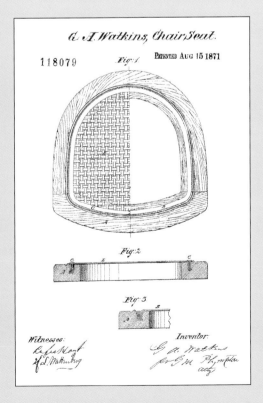

G. A. Watkins, Chair Seat.
118079   Fig. 1.   PATENTED AUG 15 1871

Fig. 2.

Fig. 3.

Witnesses: Inventor:
G. A. Watkins

Weaving the Fifth Course— The First Diagonal

Direction: from the back left corner to the front right corner.

STEP 1

Figure 5

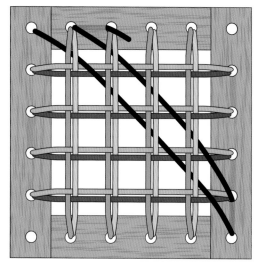

Peg the tail end of a new strand into the back left corner hole (photo 1A). Bring the strand under the vertical pair (courses 1 and 3), then over the horizontal pair (courses 2 and 4) (figure 5).

STEP 2

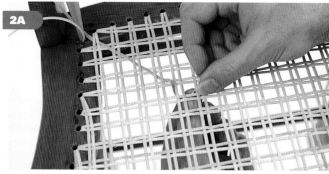

Continue toward the right front corner in this stair-step manner, going under the vertical pair and then over the horizontal pair. Keep one hand on top of the seat and the other hand underneath the seat, and pass the weaving end of the strand back and forth between hands through the larger square opening in the grid (photo 2A).

Weave one-third to one-half the way across the seat, pull up the excess, and give an extra tug to the strand. Continue weaving under the verticals and over the horizontals until there are no more verticals to go

under, then insert the cane down into the hole and up through the adjacent hole to the right (photo 2B).

The Caner's Corner

The Importance of the Proper Weaving Order

When the diagonal strand is woven correctly (B), it pulls through the weave smoothly and in a perfectly straight line. If, instead of going under the verticals and over the horizontals in this direction, you were to go over the verticals and under the horizontals (A), the diagonal would not slip into the intersections of the pairs of strands but would zigzag around them. The cane would not pull smoothly and would tend to catch and possibly break.

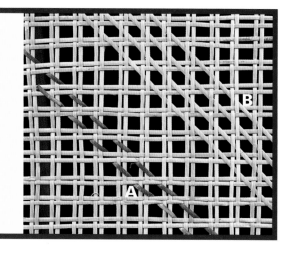

The Caner's Corner

Sometimes patterns defy logic and strands can get misplaced, throwing off the whole design. In this example (below left), the strand is coming out of the wrong hole—notice the odd contortions the strand must do to continue the weave. There is no horizontal pair for the diagonal to go over, so moving up one hole, or skipping a hole, to keep the pattern correct is the solution (below center). This last vertical row is called a short row. A rule to remember: skip the second hole below

a short row during the fifth weaving course on the right side of the chair.

When the sixth course is finished, look over what you've accomplished (below right). Notice another related rule: the diagonals will double up in the first hole below the short row on the right side of the chair during the sixth weaving course. The left side of the chair will be a mirror image of the right side of the chair.

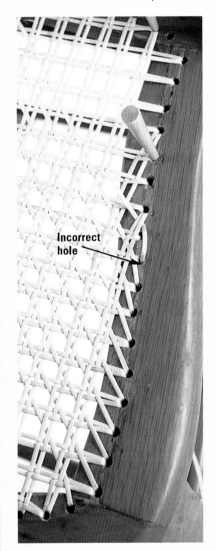

Incorrect hole

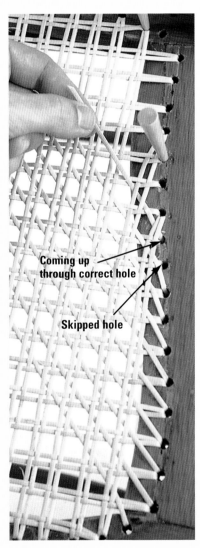

Coming up through correct hole

Skipped hole

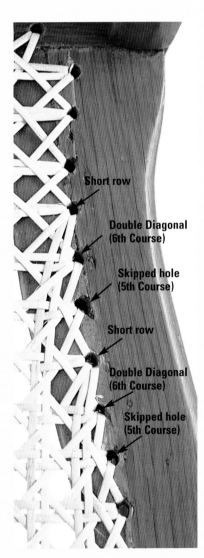

Short row

Double Diagonal (6th Course)

Skipped hole (5th Course)

Short row

Double Diagonal (6th Course)

Skipped hole (5th Course)

STEP 3

Weave over the horizontals and under the verticals to the back rail, insert the cane into the hole, and come up through the adjacent hole to the right (photo 3A).

STEP 4

Continue weaving in the same pattern down to the side rail and return to the back rail. The way the pattern of the chair used in this project was set up, the strand of cane will return to the same corner hole as long as it's woven over each horizontal and under each vertical pair in order. Weaving under the last vertical will be a little difficult. Use the caning awl to help lift the vertical pair so that you can feed the strand under it and into the hole.

You can also use the caning awl to help feed the strand under as you weave again to the front of the seat. A wire loop tool can come in handy for passing the end of the strand under the vertical pair when the intersection is over the wood of the seat (photo 4A). Remember to go over the last horizontal pair before inserting into the hole.

Weaving the Sixth Course

Direction: from back right corner to front left corner.

STEP 1

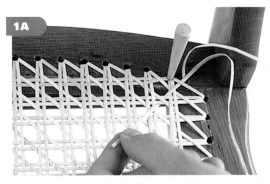

Begin weaving the sixth course by pegging the tail end of a new strand into the right rear corner hole (photo 1A). Weave under the first diagonal, if there is one, then over the vertical pair (courses 1 and 3), then under the horizontal pair (courses 2 and 4). Continue weaving across the seat in this manner.

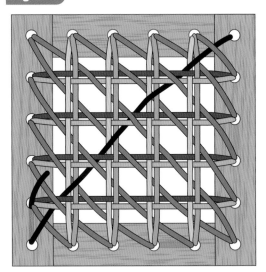
Figure 6

Everything you do during the sixth course is the mirror image of what you did during the fifth course (figure 6).

So, a rule to remember for the sixth course: skip the second hole below the short row on the left side of the chair, and your diagonals double up in the first hole below the short row on the right side of the chair.

Avoid Out of Whack Patterns, Part II

Just as there were short rows and potential pitfalls in weaving the fifth course, there can also be short rows along the front and rear seat rails as well as the side rails for the sixth course. In our example (top), notice that the second hole below the short row was not skipped, and now the diagonals are all being thrown off. They weren't woven over the last vertical pair.

When the sixth weaving course is finished and all the errors have been corrected (middle), you'll notice how uniform the series of Xs and double diagonals are (bottom), and that the diagonals are correctly doubled in the second hole below the short row. What you achieve is a professional finish around the edge of the seat.

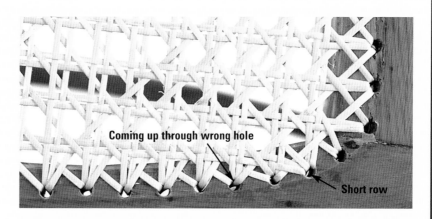

Coming up through wrong hole

Short row

Correct hole

Skipped hole

Short row

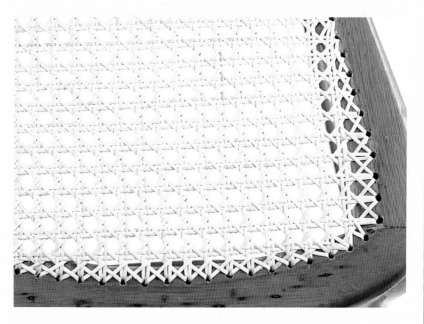

Weaving the Seventh Course

The binder step.

STEP 1

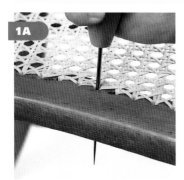

Use the caning awl to make room in each hole by carefully flattening the cane against the sides of the hole (photo 1A).

STEP 2

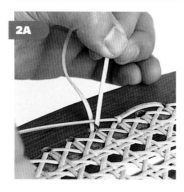

Begin the binding step near the middle of the back seat rail. Insert the end of the binder cane (which is one to two sizes larger than the weaving cane) into a hole several holes past the midway point (photo 2A). Bring the weaving cane up the outside of the middle hole, over the binding cane and back down the inside of the hole. Pull the loop tight.

STEP 3

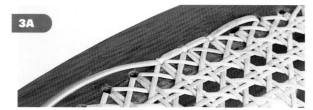

Continue looping the weaving cane up the outside of the hole, over the binding cane and down the inside of the hole. Keep the loops on the underside tight and pull the weaving cane snug enough to slightly dimple the binder cane into the hole (photo 3A).

STEP 4

Compare these two photographs (photos 4A, 4B). Take a moment to study them. In photo 4A, the binder cane is lying flat over the holes. The weaving cane is holding the binding cane in place.

However, in photo 4B, the binder cane is also lying over the holes, but the weaving cane has been pulled tighter so that the binder cane is *dimpled* into the holes. Aesthetically, this looks better and is also more structurally sound. It is less likely to catch on items during day-to-day use and cleaning.

To make the strands tight enough, it is a matter of *sawing* the weaving cane back and forth in the hole. The loop is tight when the cane is running up into the outside of the hole.

Then, as the cane is pulled down from the inside of the hole, the binder cane is lifted up to keep the tension on the upward side of the weaving cane (photos 4C, 4D). The tension on the strip of binder is loosened as the weaving strand is pulled down.

Tension on the weaving strand is held firm while the binder strip is lifted to make sure that no slack has occurred on the upward side of the weaving strand. Up and down sawing of the weaving strand and binder strip keeps the loop on the underside tight and eventually pulls the weaving strand down tight enough to dimple the binder strip.

If you wish, use the tip of a caning peg to dim-

ple the binder strip (photo 4E) to help it slip into the hole.

STEP 5

To finish the binder step, overlap the beginning and the end of the binder over two holes (photo 5A). Cut the beginning of the binder just past the second hole and then bind the two strands together in the same manner as you bound the rest of the seat.

STEP 6

Use the razor knife to carefully trim the end of the binder flush with the weaving cane that is covering it.

As you look over your freshly re-caned chair, inspect the bottom side. The loops and knots on the underside should be well spaced and neat to further indicate a job professionally done (photo 6A).

Finished classic. A reborn heirloom that's worthy of a place of honor at any table.

The Rattan Road
Rattan Harvesting and Processing

The small diameter stems (those under 20mm in diameter) must be de-thorned, usually by pulling the stem around the trunk or through the fork of a tree. Next, the outer sheath of the stem is removed revealing the shiny, green, silica-laden inner bark. The rattan stem is then cut into 30 to 40-foot lengths (9 to 12 meters). When a sufficient number of stems have been harvested they are bent in half, bundled together and the 100-pound bale is carried back to the village where the processing of the rattan begins. The large furniture rattans are cut into 12-foot (3.6 m) poles for transport.

In some areas, unprocessed rattan is shipped directly from the forest by raft or truck to processing facilities. In these cases the rattan is kept submerged underwater to prevent spoilage.

The brokers take their bales of rattan to larger ports and sell them to the representatives of the furniture industries. The Philippines, Indonesia, and Malaysia have placed prohibitions on exporting rattan at this stage of processing to protect their furniture industries. However, these policies are difficult to enforce, so a lot of rattan ends up leaving the country.

Below, left: Rattan after sulfur smoking. *Above:* Washing and scraping rattan after smoking. *Below, right:* Drying rattan in a field. Photos courtesy of David Hall, Haas School of Business, University of California Berkeley, and the P3R Organization, Kalimantan, Indonesia

THE NEEDLE CANING TECHNIQUE

As you become more familiar with the art of hand caning, and as your skills increase, you may decide to try new techniques. One common method to try is that of needle caning. This method—of two parallel settings followed by weaving the two diagonals—was first illustrated in an essay by André Jacob Roubo in the late 1760s.

Two strands are set into each hole running in one direction. A long, flat needle is used to weave the second setting, two strands at a time.

This example shows how this technique is done on a square Bergere chair, using a flat, 30-inch caning needle.

Tools and Materials

Caning needle
Set of French caning combs
    (or caning peg, tack hammer,
    or awl for straightening
    strands)

STEP 1

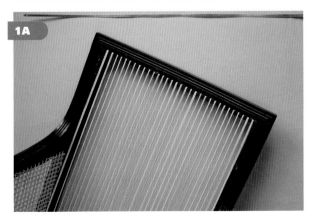

Lay in the first setting with two vertical strands (top to bottom of chair back), one strand on top of the other (photo 1A).

STEP 2

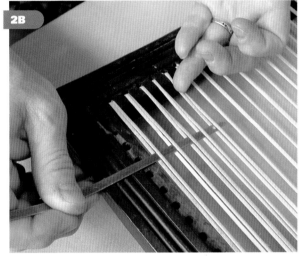

Insert the second setting with the caning needle. Before inserting the needle for the first time, it is important to separate the two vertical strands for the needle (photo 2A). Insert the needle so that

it weaves under the lower vertical and over the second (upper) vertical (photo 2B). For the first row of the second setting, insert only one strand of cane into the needle and pull it back to the left side of the chair back (photo 2C).

STEP 3

Use the caning comb, caning peg, tack hammer, or awl to push the strand into its position (photo 3A).

STEP 4

For the next row, weave the needle over the lower vertical and under the upper vertical (photos 4A).

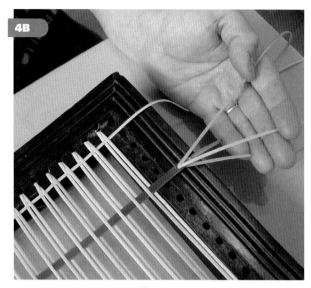

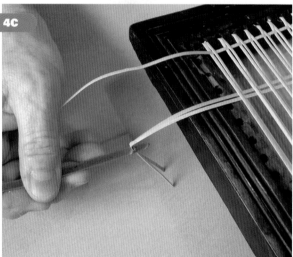

Insert two new strands of cane into the needle on the right side of the chair (photo 4B). Pull the two strands back to the left side of the chair through the weave. The two strands will be woven in the same way (photo 4C).

STEP 5

Use the comb to push one of the strands to the top of the chair back against the first strand that was woven into the back. Push the second strand to the bottom of the chair back, and insert one end of the strand into the right side hole (as you are facing the chair).

STEP 6

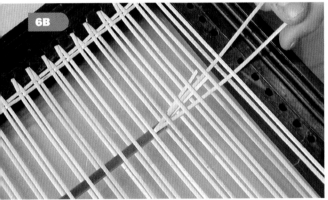

Going back to the top of the chair back, insert the strand into the top right hole—just below the corner hole—and bring the second strand up through the second hole from the corner hole (photo 6A). Weave the needle through the weave from left to right, under the first (lower) vertical strand and over the second (upper) vertical (photo 6B).

STEP 7

Insert the end of the two strands from the previous step, one strand from the top and one strand from the bottom of the chair back. Make sure that the strand has gone into the first hole from the bottom corner and out through the second hole from the bottom corner (photo 7A).

After pulling the needle back through the weave, use the comb to straighten and pack the lower pair of strands as well as the upper strand. Insert the strands into their respective holes, one strand from the top and one strand from the bottom of the chair back, and up through their adjacent holes. Now insert the needle from the opposite side to pick up these two strands and continue as before, ending in the middle, where a single strand is woven to complete the pattern.

The diagonals are woven by hand just as they were in the wooden chair used at the start of this chapter. It may help to use a shell bodkin—or wire tool—for hard-to-reach intersections.

A Victorian ladies rocker with hand-caned seat and back

Saloon chair with hand-caned seat

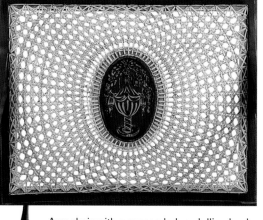

Arm chair with a suspended medallion back and hand-caned seat and detail

Detail of the seat of a bentwood stool

Detail of medallion backed arm chair

Detail of Spider Weave back on rattan rocker

Back of rattan studio chair with Snowflake pattern and detail

Gallery

European caned chair with medallion back and detail

Hand-caned ottoman

Hand-caned sunrise pattern and detail

Calla Lily chair with hand-caned seat

Chair with inlaid abalone shell and hand-caned seat

Double-caned arm chair and detail

CHAPTER 3

Natural Look and Comfort: Reworking Rush Seats

Natural rush chairs have a look and feel that's distinctly comfortable, yet refined and dignified. They're at home in any setting. Surprisingly simple, this technique has been around for ages—a testament to its popularity and unmatched functionality.

CREATING A NEW FAVORITE: REWEAVING YOUR CHAIR

irst, remove all of the old material and check to see that the chair is sound. Test all the joins to ensure that they're tight and that the seat rungs aren't loose or weak. If you detect any movement in a join, now is the time to re-glue and tighten it.

For most chairs, a 2-pound (.9 kg) coil of ⁵⁄₃₂-inch (4 mm) golden-brown fiber rush should be adequate. The slightly greenish color will age to a warm tan color within a few months. The golden-brown rush is of a better quality than the Kraft-brown colored fiber rush.

Tools and Materials

2-pound (.9 kg) coil of ⁵⁄₃₂-inch (4 mm) golden-brown fiber rush (about 400 linear feet [121.2 m])
Ruler
Pencil
Squaring tool
Rasp or coarse sandpaper
Scissors
Hammer
12 blued #3 upholstery tacks
Spring hand clamp
Large flat-head screwdriver
Pint can of 3-pound cut shellac (clear or amber), ready-to-use concentration
Paintbrush
Alcohol (for thinning shellac)

A chair for the ages. This simple ladder-backed chair and two-pound coil of rush are ready to be transformed into a functional piece of day-to-day furniture.

The Starting Line: Measuring the Corners

STEP 1

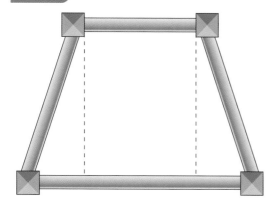

Figure 1

Before you can weave the seat, you'll have to square up the chair, or, in other words, you'll need to locate the square-shaped weaving area. In order to do that, you'll have to determine the size of the fill-in areas—or gussets—on the corners (figure 1).

Measure the length of the back seat rail, then measure the length of the front seat rail (photo 1A). If the seat is not perfectly square, the front rail will be longer than the back rail. Subtract the length of the back rail from the length of the front rail. For the chair pictured in this example, the back rail is 11½ inches (29.2 cm) and the front rail is 13½ inches (34.3 cm).

Subtracting 11½ inches (29.2 cm) from 13½ inches (34.3 cm) leaves a difference of 2 inches (5 cm). Divide this measurement in half. This gives you the amount of extra space you'll have to fill in on both corners of the front rail in order to create a square weaving area for the seat—in this case, 1 inch (2.5 cm) on both corners.

Mark 1 inch (2.5 cm) on the left side of the front rail and 1 inch (2.5 cm) on the right side of the front rail (photo 1B). The distance between the marks on the front rail should be equal to the length of the back rail. You've just squared up your chair!

Filling in the Corners, or Gussets

STEP 1

On this type of chair, you'll need to first fill in the gussets—or fill-in corners—between the front legs and the marks we made on the front rail.

Before you can begin weaving, it may be necessary to notch the outside of the two side rails. This helps keep the rush from slipping. Use the rasp or sandpaper to add notches if needed (photo 1A).

STEP 2

Cut a length of rush about 4 feet long (1.2 m). Tack one end to the side rail on the left side of the chair as the chair faces you (photo 2A). This chair will need between six and seven strands to fill in the

While there is evidence of chairs woven with rush from ancient Egypt, traditional rush seats can be traced back to 12th-century Europe, when four-legged, hand-turned chairs and stools began to appear. They were often found in churches and country homes because the materials necessary for building the chairs were very basic. With a saw, a drawknife, and a small tree sapling, all the parts of the chair could quickly be carved and assembled.

Long dried leaves, transported by the chair maker along with his few tools, were mellowed during the chair assembly process and then quickly woven into a soft, comfortable seat. The process could take as little as a day from start to finish.

Fancy rush chairs for more urbane settings differed from their country cousins with carved ornamentation on the legs, rungs, and back slats, and the use of paints for decoration. In Europe, natural rush could be round or triangular in cross-section, and could be found or cultivated around the edges of ponds. Throughout the Americas, the flat-leafed cattail, or flag, was easy to find. Even leaves and husks from corn plants or tall irises could be twisted into seats.

When exports of rattan from China were halted in the 1930s, a twisted paper fiber was developed and used for mechanized weaving of wicker fabric for Lloyd Loom furniture. The technology for manufacturing this fiber reed was used to produce fiber rush, which could be mechanically woven onto seat frames in the traditional rush style. The seat frames would later be added to the chair. When properly taken care of, these fiber rush seats would last as long as a naturally woven seat of bulrush or flag (cattail).

18th Century English Armchair,
Courtesy of The Winterthur Museum

Figure 2

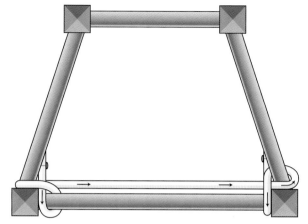

gusset. It's essential to allocate enough space along the inside of the side rails to accommodate the strands plus the beginning of the eighth strand which will go all the way around the chair. Your first tack will be very close to the front rail. The second tack will be an inch (2.5 cm) or so back, and so on (figure 2) .

STEP 3

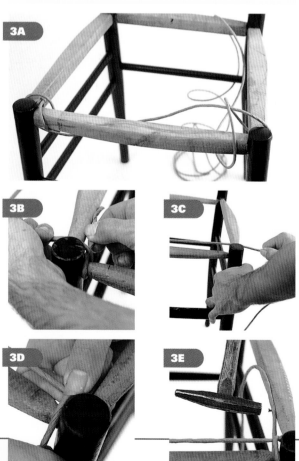

After tacking the rush to the inside of the side rail, bring the rush over the front rail, around the front rail, up and over the left side rail, around the left side rail, across the seat and over the right side rail (photo 3A). Then bring it around the right side rail, up and over the front rail at the right corner, around the front rail, and clamp it to the right side rail where it will be tacked after the strand is pulled taut (photos 3B, 3C, 3D, 3E).

STEP 4

It's important to tighten the strands in the proper order. Go back to the left side of the chair and pull the strand taut, from the tack to the top of the front rail. Make sure the rush is twisting uniformly, without any kinks, then pull straight down and under the front rail, then up and over to the left side rail. Before pulling the strand tight, hold the run of the strand as it is going from the tack to the front rail with the thumb and index finger of your right hand, so that the strand cannot move sideways.

With your left hand, bring the strand from under the front rail and across the run you're holding with your right hand, and bring it over the left side rail. As the two strands cross each other, pinch the two strands together with your right thumb and index finger. Hold the two strands so that the first run doesn't move and pull from the pinch to the edge of the left side rail.

Bring the strand around the left side rail and then across the seat to the right side rail. Turn the chair so that you are pulling toward your stomach. (Turn the chair at every corner so you always pull toward yourself. It will help keep the tension uniform.) Pull the strand taut, go over the right side rail, then under and up from behind and grab the run from the left side rail between the thumb and index finger of your right hand, as you did before.

Holding the strand that came from across the seat so that it remains in the same position, bring the other end of the strand from below the right seat rail, over the strand you're holding and the front seat rail.

As the two strands cross each other, pinch the two strands together and hold them in place. Pull from the pinch to the front seat rail. Bring the strand underneath the front rail, pull it to the right side rail and tack the end into the side rail, near the front corner. (Remember to allow room for tacking five or six more strands to this side rail.) Cut off the excess strand about an inch (2.5 cm) from the tack.

STEP 5

Attach a second strand to the left side rail about an inch (2.5 cm) behind the first tack, making sure that you are making the proper allowance for the six or seven more strands that will be tacked to this rail. Follow the same process as before for each strand until the gussets are filled. Check to make sure that strands are crossing at right angles (photo

5A). Use a screwdriver or a block of wood and a hammer to tap the individual strands to keep the strands at right angles to each other (photo 5B). Do this each time you complete two to three rows.

Weaving and Stuffing the Chair

STEP 1

Figure 3

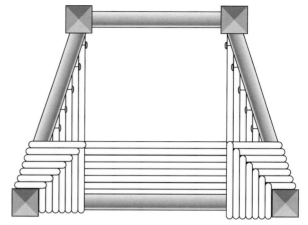

When the fill-in strands reach the mark you made on the front rail (1 inch (2.5 cm) on this chair), the gusset is complete (figure 3) and now we can begin weaving around the entire chair seat. Tack the end of a 20 to 30-foot (6 to 9 m) length of rush to the back corner of the left side rail and pull it to the

top of the front rail (photo 1A). Weave it over and around as you did with the fill-in strands, except instead of finishing it off on the right rail, take it back to the rear seat rail, wrap it over and around

Figure 4

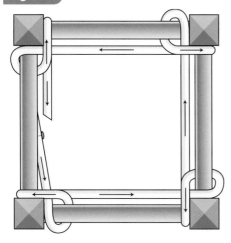

and then to the rear of the right side rail, over and around to the opposite rail, then around and over the rear side rail heading back to the front rail (figure 4).

The *Caner's* Corner

Joining Two Strands

When you run out of rush, join a new 20 to 30-foot (6 to 9 m) strand with a square knot to the end of the strand you've been weaving. Make sure the knot falls along the run between two woven corners so that it will be hidden from view as the seat progresses. After you've tied and tightened the knot, trim the ends.

STEP 2

2A

For the first full course, weave the rush loosely around all the corners, then tighten each corner individually. Always make your corners by controlling where the strand lays (photo 2A). Pinch the two strands together and pull taut from where you're holding the strands together. Don't let the strand parallel to the run move toward the rail as you pull the strand over the chair rail. Be sure to keep the intersections of strands at right angles.

STEP 3

3A

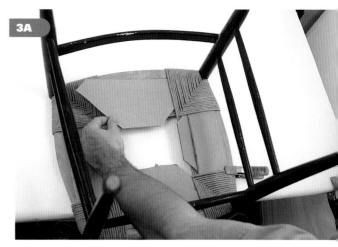

After you have woven about a third of the seat, it's time to start stuffing the chair. It's better to stuff the bottom first (photo 3A) so the top will be flat. If you only stuff the top of the seat, the seat will be puffier than if the bottom is stuffed as well.

High-quality corrugated cardboard tends to work best and will likely give you the best results. Cut the cardboard in triangular shapes so it will fit

neatly between the layers of the weave. Make sure that the corrugations of the cardboard run parallel to the chair rail so the cardboard won't buckle while being inserted (photos 3B, 3C). Blunt the

corners so that they don't fold back on themselves as you push the cardboard into place (photo 3D). In this example, the next layer uses smaller pieces of cardboard. Be sure to cut in the same shape. The purpose is to get a smooth layering that fills in any loose space in the weave.

STEP 4

Continue weaving and stuffing the chair. Periodically, tap the strands over with the large screwdriver and hammer to keep the strands at right angles to each other (photo 4A). Measure the dis-

tance between the strands at the chair rail as well as at the opening in the center to make sure that the strands are parallel to each other. If they are not, tap the strand over until the two strands are parallel.

Before the sides close up, tie a new strand of rush that is long enough to finish weaving the chair seat (photo 4B). Make sure the knot is tied in a place where it will be hidden and that you trim the ends of the knot.

STEP 5

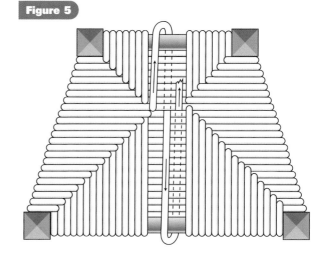

To fill in the last of the pattern, a figure-eight weaving pattern is used. This is called the bridge. It starts at either the front or back rail, depending on which direction the rush is heading (figure 5).

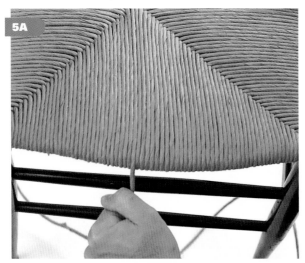

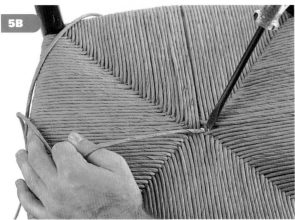

Bring the strand up, over, around, and underneath the rail. Pull the strand up through the center hole (photos 5A, 5B) in the direction of the opposite rail, either front or back depending on the direction you were heading. Repeat this until the figure eight is completed. When the last bit of space on the rails is filled, turn the chair over and tack the rush to the underside of the nearest rail (photo 5C).

STEP 6

Cut the strand 3 to 4 inches (7.6 to 10.2 cm) from the tack, unravel the strand, and hide the end of the strand in the weave on the underside of the seat (photo 6A). Burnish the strands into place by rolling the handle of the screwdriver on top of the seat (photo 6B).

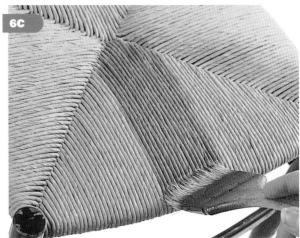

When you're done, seal your new rush seat with a thinned coat of clear or amber shellac (photo 6C).

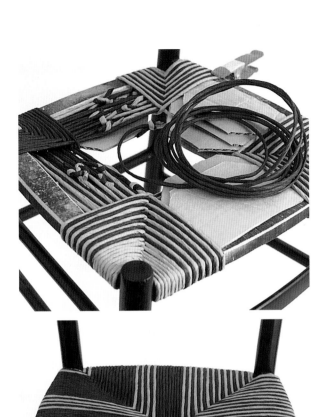

Other Styles And Techniques

With paper rush, a new color can be introduced to the weave and design by cutting the previous colored strand and tying a new colored strand in place (see photos at left). When you try these types of patterns, make sure the knots all fall in the run area, and try to stagger the knots so that they are not all in the same position in the run.

The Caner's Corner

Taking Care of a Rush Seat

Now that you've invested your time in weaving a beautiful seat, you'll want it to last as long as possible. By doing a good job of weaving a tight seat with the cardboard stuffing covering the wooden edge of the chair seat, you've protected the seat from being cut from the inside. The shellac will protect the outside surface of the seat. But as the chair seat is used, the finish coat will wear away.

It is important to renew the finish coat every couple of years or so, depending on the use and the seat's exposure to sunlight. If the chairs are in a sunny room, you might want to renew the finish every year.

You can also use a full-strength (not thinned) coat of shellac; the seat finish will be shinier than the thinned coat. You may also use varnish or varathane if you prefer it to shellac. Once again, if the finish is used straight from the can, it will have a more plastic look than if you thin down the finish to make it more natural.

Gallery

Windsor rocker with a fiber rush seat

Ladder-back style chair with a fiber rush seat

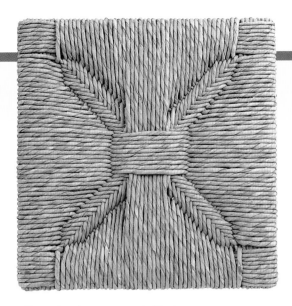

Natural rush seat woven in Mexico

Contemporary
stool with a fiber
rush seat

Hans Wegner
"Wishbone Chair"

CHAPTER 4

Splint Weaving Techniques for Down-Home Comfort

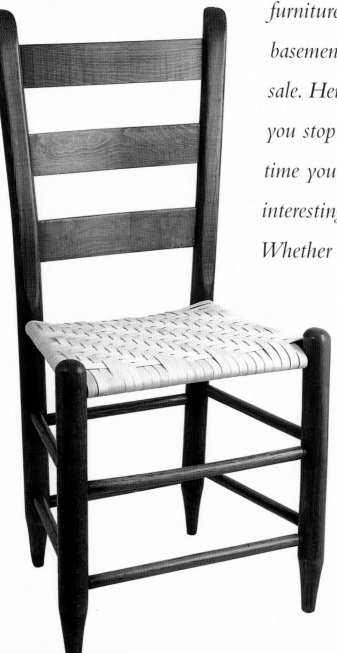

Everyone has seen forgotten pieces of furniture here and there—in a garage or basement, or at a neighborhood yard sale. Here's a technique that will make you stop and take special notice the next time you stumble across a humble yet interesting chair, stool, or footstool. Whether it was originally manufactured for splint or not, chances are it can be brought back to life with a simple-to-do splint weave.

GETTING STARTED WITH SPLINT: LEARN THE BASICS ON A SIMPLE FOOTSTOOL

T he footstool pictured in this project is a fairly common find. It was likely manufactured with either a rush seat or a woven seat with wide binder cane. Working on an item like this is a great way to learn a basic splint weaving technique. The seat is rectangular so there are no corner gussets to fill in. To begin, you'll set up the long sides with the spaced warp strands (the strands you actually weave around and through), and then weave over and under three strands at a time.

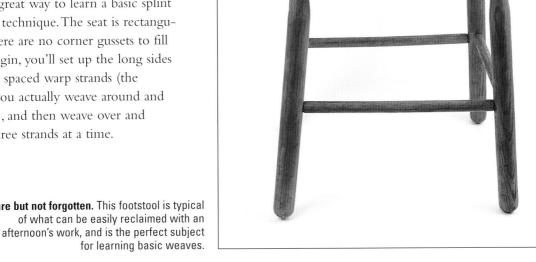

Bare but not forgotten. This footstool is typical of what can be easily reclaimed with an afternoon's work, and is the perfect subject for learning basic weaves.

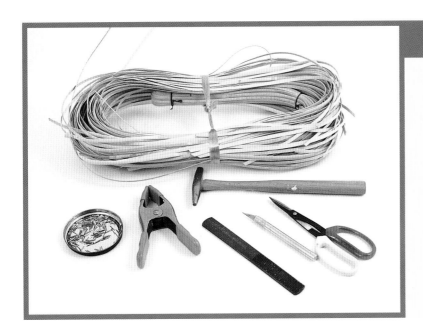

Tools and Materials

Wood glue
Hand spring clamp
Rasp or coarse sandpaper
500-foot hank of 6-8 mm
   binder cane
Scissors
Large bowl of hot water
1 dozen ½-inch
   (1.3 cm) x 20-gauge wire nails
Tack hammer
Awl or ice pick
Hobby knife
Table knife (non-serrated)

Starting Point

Make sure the stool frame is secure and that all joins are tight. If anything is loose, now is the time to glue the frame back together, using wood clamps. Be sure that all four feet rest on the floor. It's also a good time to see if the seat rails have a sharp inner edge. If so, this will end up cutting the cane from the inside when the stool is used. Use the rasp or sandpaper on the inner edge to round it off.

Setting Up the Warp Strands

Start by soaking a few strands of 6 to 8 mm binder cane in hot water. Soak one or two strands at a time for approximately 15 minutes. If cane is over-soaked it will turn a greenish/gray color and will not blend

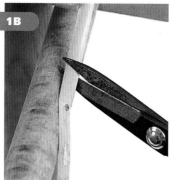

with the light, cream color of the other strands. Place one end of the strand against the shorter side rail, and attach it to the rail with a ½-inch (1.3 cm) x 20-gauge wire nail (photo 1A). Come back about 3 inches (7.6 cm) from the end of the cane to put the nail in. If you try to put a nail in the end of the strand, the strand will split. After the nail is set, trim the end of the cane closer to the nail location (photo 1B).

STEP 2

Bring the strand under and around the closer seat rail and over the opposite rail. Continue to bring the strand back to the closer rail, around this rail, and then over the opposite rail a second time. Use a hand-clamp to hold the strand in place on the opposite rail (photo 2A).

STEP 3

Insert the decorative binding strip at this point. This strand serves two purposes: not only is it a decorative element, it also functions structurally to preserve the warp strands that go across the seat. Insert 1 to 2 inches (2.5 to 5 cm) of the end of a 24-inch (61 cm) length of 6-8 mm binder cane, with the shiny side down, under the two warp strands that cross the open seat area. Fold the strand to the right so that it covers the pair of warp strands (photo 3A).

Duplicate this on the other rail by adding a 24-inch (61 cm) strip of binder. Again, insert it with the shiny side down, about an inch or two (2.5 to 5 cm), under the two warp strands. Fold the strand to the right so that it covers the pair of warp strands.

STEP 4

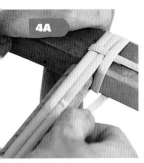

Before bringing the warp strand back to the closer rail, wrap the strand around the opposite rail and the decorative strip two times (photo 4A), then place a clamp on the

wrap. Bring the strand to the closer rail and wrap it around the close rail one time (photo 4B) then a second time. Do not worry that the pattern is not the same on the bottom as it is on the top. If you'd like to check ahead and look at the photos of the bottom of the seat as the weave progresses, you'll see that it all works out okay.

After wrapping around the close rail and the decorative strip two times, bring the

warp strand *under* the decorative strip and across to the opposite seat rail, bringing the warp strand *under* the decorative strip on that side as well (photo 4C).

The Caner's Corner

Joining a New Strand

When you come to the end of the strand, the easiest place to join a new strand to the old one is during the double wrap around the seat rail and the decorative strip. You will want to join the strands while wrapping the strand two times around the rail. Place the tail end of the new strand against the rail as you wrap one time around with the end of the old strand, so that one wrap catches and holds the tail end of the new strand.

Twist the old and new strands once around each other so that the new strand becomes the wrapping strand and the old strand is folded against the rail. You'll trim this tailpiece later. Finish the second wrap with the new strand, making sure the twist is flat against the rail.

STEP 5

Wrap around the side rail and decorative wrap two times, then across to the opposite side. Wrap twice around the rail and the decorative

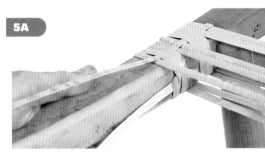

wrap then bring the strand under the decorative wrap. Continue setting the warp strands and wrapping as before (photo 5A): wrap twice around the full width of the seat rails, followed by two wraps around the individual rail, far side first, then the near side, followed by two more wraps around the full width of the rails.

STEP 6

Before tightening the last two warp strands, tuck the ends of the decorative strip into a loop with the end coming out at the previous pair (photo 6A). Use a sponge or rag to moisten the loop with hot water so that it is very flexible. Leave enough room in the loop to fit the last two strands. After weaving the last two strands through the loop, and while tightening them, pull the loop tight. You might use an awl or ice pick to help keep the loop formed and flat as you pull it tight.

The pattern should finish out symmetrically, but if it doesn't, an extra wrap or two on both rails is okay. Trim the ends of the decorative binder strip with a hobby knife (photo 6B).

STEP 7

To end the warping strand, tack it to the bottom of the side rail. In this project, the stool's warp strand was a tad too short, so I had to add an extra length by nailing the start and finish of the last warp strand to the underside of the rail (photo 7A). The weaving strands will cover this join.

When everything in this step is done and you're satisfied at the way everything looks, trim the ends with the hobby knife. The remaining tail ends will be hidden inside the seat.

The Weaving Steps

This is where you'll begin weaving the seat. In order to save time—and to keep from having to flip the stool over every time you finish one side—weave with three strands at a time. This will cause the weaving on the bottom of the seat to be slightly diagonal, but that's a common occurrence.

STEP 1

Weave one strand from right to left, going over a pair of warp strands, then under the next pair of warp strands, then over the next pair, and so on until you get to the left side of the seat (photo 1A). Pull the strand to the left so that you have about 18 inches (46 cm) of the weaver hanging over on the left side.

Weave a second strand from right to left, but this time go under a pair of warp strands, then over, then under so that this strand weaves just the opposite to the first strand (photo 1B). Pull this strand to the left so that you have about 18 inches (46 cm) of the second weaver hanging over on the left side. Use your fingers to push or comb the strands tightly together.

Weave a third strand from right to left, in the same manner as you wove the first strand. Leave about 18 inches (46 cm) of this third strand hanging over on the left side.

STEP 2

Turn the stool over so that the short ends are to the left and the long weavers are to the right. Weave in the first short strand across the bottom of the seat, but at a slight angle so that the strand weaves across some of the wood of the seat rail (photo 2A).

Weave in the second short strand across the bottom in the same over/under pattern as the first short strand, also at a diagonal. Weave in the third short strand across the bottom in the same over/under pattern as the first and second short strand, also at a diagonal. Leave the ends of these strands out. You'll trim them after you see how well the weaving on the bottom goes.

Take the long end of the first weaver and weave it from right to left in the opposite weaving pattern of the three strands you've just completed. Adjust the strands so that they lay against each other in a pleasing fashion. Remember that the weavers across

the bottom will end up at a slight diagonal, while the weaving on the top of the seat will be perpendicular to the warp.

Take the long end of the second weaver and weave it from right to left in the same weaving pattern as the previous strand (photo 2B).

STEP 3

Turn the stool upright and continue the weaving pattern you've established in the previous steps (photo 3A).

STEP 4

When you've woven about one half of the bottom of the seat, you'll have to adjust the weaving by one strand to account for the change in the warp structure. This is just a one-time adjustment. The last complete set of three strands, from left to right, go under two, over two, under two, and so on (photo 4A). The next strand (being held in the photo), goes from left to right, over one, under two, over two, under two and so on. The rest of the strands will follow this new pattern.

Adding a New Weaver

When it is time to add a new weaver, make your additions on the bottom of the seat. Trim the end of the retiring strand so that it is a tad shorter than the woven portion of the seat. The new strand will lie directly over the end of the old strand. The overlap should be a minimum of 8 inches (20.3 cm). The friction of the weave will keep the strands from slipping after the weaving is completed.

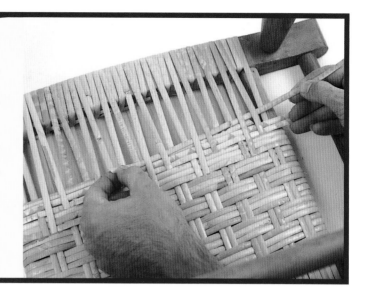

STEP 5

As you get close to the end of the weaving it will be harder to manipulate the weaving strand over and under without the use of a tool. The blade of a dinner knife can help at this point if you slip it under a pair of warp strands from the opposite side that you are trying to insert the weaver. Insert the blade from one side, and slip the weaver between the knife blade and the warp to feed it through. Pull the knife out and back up to the next pair the weaver will go under, and use it to guide the weaver. Using this technique will save you a lot of wear and tear on your fingers.

As you finish up your weaving, fold the end of the weaving strand back underneath the nearest warp strand to lock the weaver into place (photo 5A).

5A

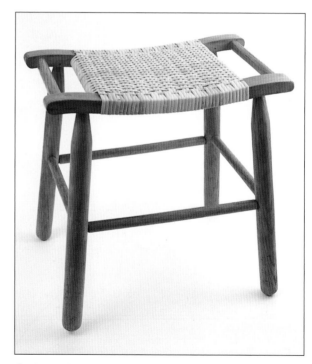

Getting underfoot. This finished footstool is ready for use.

REKINDLE YOUR RUSTIC SPIRIT: SPLINT WEAVING CHAIRS

Weaving with splint is simple to do and very quick to complete. Any chair or stool with four dowels for seat frame rails can be splint woven. The weaving pattern itself is a simple basket weave similar to that done by children weaving construction paper place mats. Splint seats are exceptionally strong and very durable when properly cared for.

The Herringbone Seat Pattern

When weaving a country splint seat we actually weave two panels at the same time: the first seat is on top of the chair; the second is on the underside of the first seat with a space between the two woven panels.

This project illustrates how to weave the herringbone splint seat pattern, a technique commonly found on country chairs or obviously handmade chairs. All the tools needed for splint weaving can be found in most homes. The materials are available through many suppliers. Oak, hickory, ash, and reed splints are generally stocked, although their supply can be irregular. When inquiring about splint, be sure to ask what widths are available.

The amount of splint you'll need will vary according to the size of the seat you're trying to cover. The chart on this page can help you in determining how much material you'll need.

Flat reed, which is most commonly used in splint weaving, is the inner core of the rattan palm cut flat or slightly oval. The easiest way to determine which side is the top and which is the bottom is to bend the reed into a loop. If small splinters (or hairs) are raised at the point of the bend, then you're looking at the underside of the reed.

Binder cane is cut from the peel or bark of the rattan palm. It is available only in millimeter widths, and are usually labeled narrow (4 mm), medium (5 mm), wide (6 mm), and extra-wide (7 to 8 mm).

Size of Seat	Amount of ½-inch splint	Amount of ⅝-inch splint	Amount of 1-inch splint
13 x 10 in. (33 x 25.4 cm)	84 ft. (25.6 m)	72 ft. (22 m)	42 ft. (12.8 m)
15 x 12 in. (38.1 x 30.5 cm)	120 ft. (36.6 m)	102 ft. (31.1 m)	60 ft. (18.3 m)
18 x 14 in. (45.7 x 35.6 cm)	156 ft. (47.6 m)	132 ft. (40.2 m)	78 ft. (23.8 m)
19 x 16 in. (48.3 x 40.6 cm)	198 ft. (60.4 m)	168 ft. (51.2 m)	99 ft. (30.2 m)
21 x 17 in. (53.3 x 43.2 cm)	228 ft. (69.5 m)	192 ft. (58.5 m)	114 ft. (34.8 m)
22 x 19 in. (55.9 x 48.3 cm)	252 ft. (76.8 m)	213 ft. (64.9 m)	126 ft. (38.4 m)

Rural Route
Splint Seating: A Natural History

Even though the lathe dates back to ancient Egypt, it was in the 12th century that a more efficient form of the turning lathe was devised. Greenwood chair building became more refined because wood could be shaped faster. Also, decorative elements of a simple chair could be carved while on the lathe, simplifying the ornamentation process.

The structure of a basic turned wood chair— with four seat rails—lets the maker use either a board for a seat, or one made of leather or fabric attached to the seat rails. It also allowed for the innovation of a seat woven over and around the seat rails.

Several European trees—elm, ash, and chestnut—have wood grain that splits into long, uniform strips. These were used to interlace a simple basket weave pattern around the seat rails. As skill in trimming the wood splints increased and thinner weaving elements became available, varieties of patterns, including complex variations of twill patterns, emerged. Basketry willow might have also been used to weave the seats of these turned chairs, but probably not until the 17th century.

Once rattan was introduced to the Colonies, wider cane began to be used to weave the lathe-turned chair seats. One manufacturer, Old Hickory Chair Company, used a combination of hickory bark and wide rattan peel (cane) on seats and backs of the noble furniture that adorn most of the lodges in America's National Parks.

In the southeastern United States, splint seats were woven with hickory bark and white oak, while black or brown ash was the preferred

Hickory arm chair with checkerboard seat, Old Hickory Chair Company

seating material throughout the Northeast. Fur trappers used rawhide for chair seats in Canada and along the Mississippi River.

The Shakers used 1 and 2-inch-wide (2.5 and 5 cm) cotton webbing to weave the seats and backs of their traditional chairs and stools. When commercially made materials became affordable, splints made from the inner core of rattan or rattan peel were frequently substituted for the more expensive and hard-to-find ash, white oak, and hickory bark weavers.

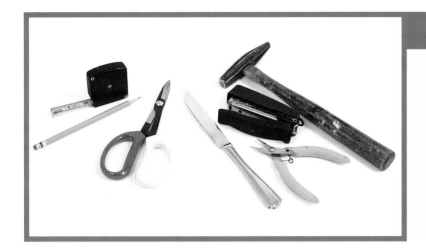

½-inch (1.3 cm) flat reed splint
Tape measure
Floral shears
Pencil
Spring hand clamps
Desk stapler
Tack hammer
Table knife (non-serrated)
Needle-nose pliers

Getting Started

Before you start with any of the various materials you can use for splint weaving, you should always soak them in hot water for approximately five or 10 minutes. Be careful not to over-soak them, otherwise they may expand too much or become discolored and hairy.

In this project, the chair pictured is called a *mule eared* side chair (the name comes from the shape of the tops of the leg posts). Because the front rail is longer than the back rail, several fill-in lengths will be needed to cover the extra spaces in the corners, called gussets.

Simple and stately. The secret to weaving this mule-eared chair is in measuring and filling the gussets.

Measuring the Seat Area

Measure the length of the back seat rail (above), then measure the length of the front seat rail. Subtract the length of the back rail from the length of the front rail. The distance between the back posts along the seat rail is 10½ inches (26.7 cm). The distance between the front leg posts along the seat rail is 14 inches (35.6 cm).

Subtracting 10½ inches (26.7 cm) from 14 inches (35.6 cm) leaves a difference of 3½ inches (8.9 cm). Divide this measurement in half, or 1¾ inches (4.4 cm). This is the amount of extra space you'll have to fill on both corners of the front rail in order to create a square weaving area for the seat.

Measure and mark 1¾ inches (4.4 cm) on the left side of the front rail and on the right side of the front rail. The distance between the marks on the front rail should be equal to the length of the back rail.

STEP 1

Find out which is the top side and underside of the splint. Turn the wet splint into a tight bend. One side will be *hairy*, while the other side will be smooth. Always weave the flat reed splint so that the hairy side is toward the inside of the seat (photos 1A, 1B).

Begin *warping* the seat by tacking or tying the end of the flat reed to the inside of the back seat rail. Bring the flat reed under and around the left

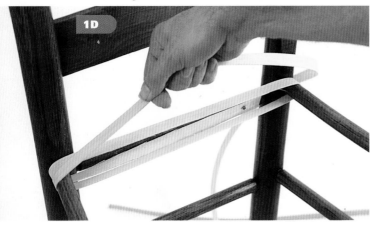

rail to the top of the seat, then across and around the right rail (photo 1C). Continue around the right rail and across the bottom of the seat, returning to the left side (photo 1D). Continue warping the seat until you reach the end of the strand.

STEP 2

On the chair in our illustration, the first warp strand wraps around the right seat rail leaving about a 10-inch (25.4 cm) tail on the underside of the seat (photo 2A).

This is perfect. You'll want all the joins to be on the underside of the seat with an overlap of 6 to 8 inches (15.2 to 20.3 cm). Use a spring clamp to hold the tail in position.

STEP 3

Check the new strand for the right and wrong side, and with the wrong side facing up into the center of the seat, overlap it with the tail of the original warp strand 6 to 8 inches (15.2 to 20.3 cm). Use a common desk stapler and staple the two strands together at three places, 2 inches (5 cm) apart (photo 3A). Make sure the prongs of the staples aim toward the center of the seat so that only the heads of the staples are visible from the underside of the seat. This will protect your hands if you brush against the staples and will make it easy to remove any visible staples when we're finished weaving the seat.

Continue warping the seat with the new strand. Continue joining strands in the same manner until there is no more room along the side rails to add another warp strand.

Tack or tie the end of the strand to the inside of the front seat rail (photo 3B).

Weaving The Seat

STEP 1

Now that the chair is set with warp strands, you can begin to weave the seat. After checking the right and wrong sides of the strand, weave a new strand of splint from front to back using the following weaving pattern: over three strands, under three strands, over three strands, under three strands, until you reach the back rail of the chair seat (photo 1A). If the last pattern is only under or over one or two, that's okay; each chair will be different.

You should leave a 12 to 14-inch (30.5 to 35.6 cm) tail hanging down from the front of the seat while the rest of the weaving strand hangs down in back of the chair (photo 1B).

STEP 2

Turn the chair over. First we'll weave the tail into the warp strands on the bottom of the seat (photo 2A). Weave the same pattern as on the top: over three strands, under three strands, over three strands, and so on, until you reach the back chair leg. Cut the end of the strand if it sticks out past the chair leg.

Now, studying the pattern you just wove with the tail, weave the end of the long strand from the back over and under three strands so that the weave makes a *step up* from the adjacent strand. Pull the strand snug. (Take a look at the weaving pattern diagram [figure 1] for more details. It will help you determine how best to count strands in a way that's suitable to the chair you're reweaving. Please see Appendix B (page 118) for a diagram illustrating the popular diamond weaving pattern shown in the photograph on page 84.)

Figure 1

Weaving pattern diagram showing the staggered "step up" over-three/under-three diamond weave.

STEP 3

Turn the chair over and weave over two strands, under three strands, over three strands, under three strands. Make sure the first weaving strand is aligned against the pencil mark (photo 3A). The second weaver should be stepped down one strand (photo 3B).

STEP 4

Turn the chair over and weave across the bottom of the seat, continuing the stepped pattern (photo 4A).

When it is time to add a new strand, overlap the new strand over the old strand 6 to 8 inches (15.2 to 20.3 cm) making sure that both strands are woven identically.

Trim the old strand just short of the front rail (photo 4B). Align the two strands in the weave. You don't need to staple these splices. The friction of the weave will hold the strands in place.

Continue weaving across the top of the seat—don't pull the new strand too taut or you'll pull it out of the weave. Keep weaving the stepped pattern until the strand brushes up against the inside of the back post (photo 4C). You can adjust the strands along the back rail to some degree to fit this last strand in.

STEP 5

Bring the strand around the rail, weave across the bottom of the seat, and continue across the top of the seat. This strand should now be on the right side of the pencil mark you made on the rail. You are now filling in the gusset on the right. Weave the strand over three and under three until you can weave no more. Cut the strand short of the rail and tuck it into the weave (photos 5A, 5B).

5C

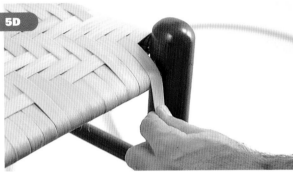

5D

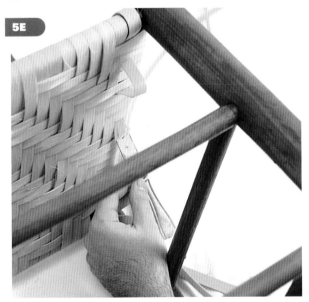

5E

Cut as many short strands as necessary to finish weaving the gusset. Weave one or more strands on the top to fill in the gusset, then weave the other ends into the bottom of the seat. Use the table knife to help slide the weavers into position (photos 5C, 5D, 5E).

STEP 6

6A

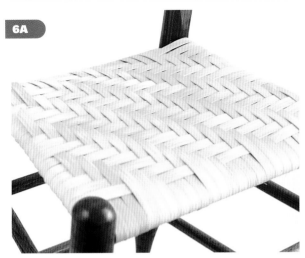

Finish the seat by filling in the gusset on the left side of the chair. Turn the chair over and fit as many strands as necessary into the weave on the bottom of the seat. Turn the chair over again and weave these strands into the top of the seat (photo 6A). Make sure you continue to follow the stepped pattern.

Finally, use the needle nose-pliers to remove any visible staples on the bottom of the seat.

Wonderful rustic charm. This finished mule-eared chair is destined to be a comfortable family favorite for years to come.

Gallery

Example of woven diamond pattern

Side chair with double side rail by influential and innovative Danish designer Hans Wegner

Shaker armchair. Woven cotton Shaker tape woven on seat and back

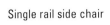
Single rail side chair

Walnut stool with twill woven splint seat of hickory bark. Stool by Oscar Hensley

Danish folding chair with binder cane woven seat and back

"The Chair" by Hans Wegner

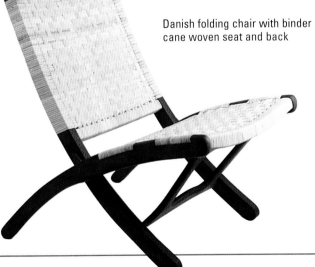

CHAPTER 5

Wound Up for Wicker

Repairing wicker can be a rewarding craft in and of itself. Wickerwork uses basketry techniques, but on a larger scale and adapted to the structure of furniture. With a little patience and skill, you can transform a derelict bundle of twigs into an intricate woven piece of furniture possessing both structural strength and old-world charm.

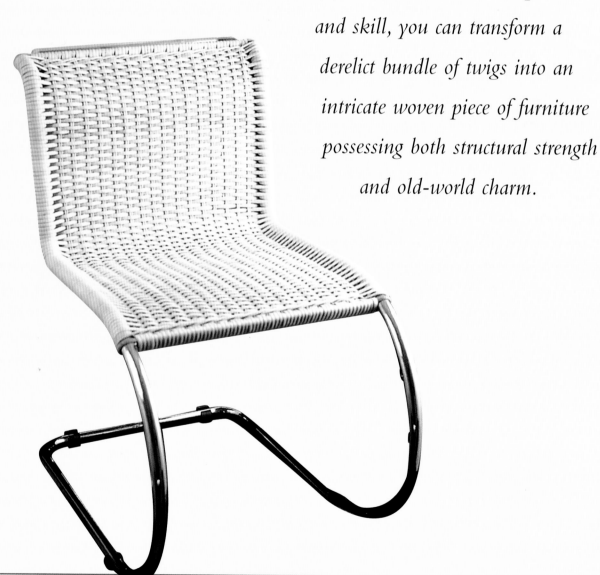

RECLAIM A MODERN CLASSIC: THE LUDWIG MIES VAN DER ROHE CHAIR

This project—reweaving a classic chair designed by Ludwig Mies Van Der Rohe—reveals the structure and technique behind most wicker furniture. By weaving onto a tubular steel framework you'll see that nails, tacks, and glue are unnecessary. The caner's skill of interweaving and wrapping rattan (flat oval reed and round reed) will produce a beautiful, strong, and striking result.

Getting Started

This particular chair has two lengths of flat steel welded at the top and bottom of the woven area. This is a redesign of the original chair frame which had two pieces of wood that were in the same location but were held in place by the two pieces of split rattan and the wrapping. The split rattan on this chair is purely decorative (below).

Bare essentials. The tubular structure of this chair designed by Ludwig Mies Van Der Rohe provides a sturdy frame for wicker weaving.

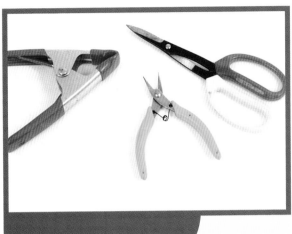

Tools and Materials

Masking tape
16 strands of #5 (3.25 mm) round reed,
   96 inches (244 cm) long, folded in half
2 coils (2 lb [.9 kg]) of ¼-inch (6 mm)
   flat oval reed
2 lengths of whole rattan split in half,
   10 mm in diameter
Round-nose pliers
Spring hand clamp

STEP 1

Wrap one layer of masking tape around the sharp curves at the top of the chair (photo 1A). This will help the weaving stay in place as you work around the sharp curve of the frame. The split rattan has been cut to encompass the steel rod and the tubular framework. The ends butt together on the underside of the flat steel rod. The holes in the steel rod were used to support the frame while it was put through the chrome process.

1A

Cut one 48-inch (122 cm) strand of round reed and lay the end of the strand against the middle of the inside edge of the top, flat piece of steel. Tuck the end of a very long length of ¼-inch flat oval reed against the top steel piece and begin wrapping around the end of the round reed, the end of the length of flat oval, and the steel piece. Wrap two or three times around the reed, then one wrap behind the piece of reed.

STEP 2

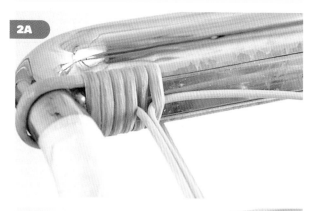

Take a 96-inch (244 cm) length of round reed and fold it in half. Lay one half of the strand against the first spoke you've just wrapped into place, and wrap around the new spoke to hold it. Wrap two more times around the new spoke then once *behind* it (photos 2A, 2B).

Take another 96-inch (244 cm) length of round reed, fold it in half, lay one half of the strand against the second spoke that you've wrapped into place, and wrap around the new spoke to hold it (photo 2C). Continue wrapping three times around the middle of the length of reed, once behind, three

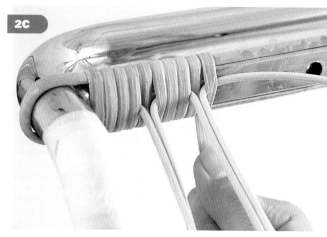

wraps around, one wrap behind, and so on, until all sixteen pairs of spokes have been wrapped and anchored to the top of the weaving frame. Add a new strand if needed to complete the wrap.

Tuck the end of the wrapping strand back through two wraps and pull it tight. Try to have the wrap end just underneath the last spoke. Make sure the spokes are all centered along the frame and coming straight forward from the frame in line with the profile of the chair frame. (NOTE: There can be variations in the width of the flat oval reed, and you might end up with 15 or even 17 pairs of spokes. Don't worry. Just keep the spacing uniform and the spokes parallel.)

STEP 3

The next step is a *three-rod twining* step. Wrap a long length of round reed twice around the left side of the chair. Bring one strand under the first pair of spokes and up. Bring the other end of the strand

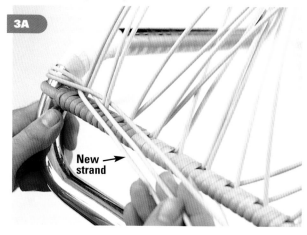

New strand

over the first pair of spokes and under the second pair of spokes. Take a new strand and insert it between the chair frame and the first pair of spokes (photo 3A). This strand should also be between the wrapping and strand that went over the first pair of spokes.

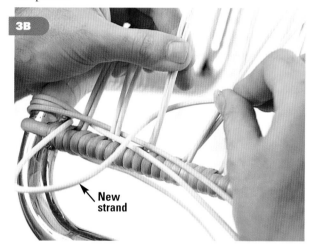

Take this new strand closest to the chair frame, bring it over the first two pairs of spokes and behind the third pair (photo 3B). Pull the weaver snug, but not tight.

Now take the weaver farthest to the left and bring it over the next two pairs of spokes and behind the fourth pair. Pull this weaver snug, but not tight.

Again, take the weaver still farthest to the left and bring it over the next two pairs of spokes and behind the fifth pair (photo 3C). Pull this weaver snug, but not tight.

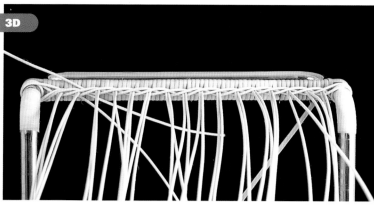

Continue weaving from the left to the right (looking down on the back of the chair) until you've woven once across the back. To finish the weave, bring the weavers around the frame and back into the weave (photo 3D).

Weaving the Seat

STEP 1

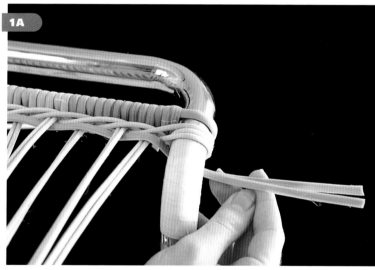

Take two strands of ¼-inch (6 mm) flat oval reed and put the flat sides together and weave over one pair of spokes, then under the next pair of spokes, then over, under, and so on (photo 1A). Leave a tail of a few inches of the weaver at the beginning.

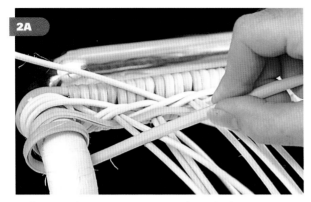

When you've woven across and reach the opposite side of the frame, wrap the double weaver once completely around the frame and then weave back in the opposite direction. Don't just wrap around the frame, but go completely around it—like you're doing one and three-quarter wraps (photo 2A).

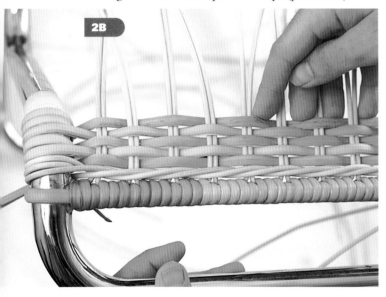

Continue weaving back and forth. Make sure that in one direction the weave is going over, under, over, and so on. In the return direction, the weave should be just the opposite. Use your fingers to keep the row of weavers flat against the preceding row (photo 2B).

The Caner's Corner

Controlling Spokes During Weaving

In all weaving, the weft's purpose is to hold the warp strands—in this case, the spokes—in position. Weavers are not pulled tight, but they should be somewhat snug.

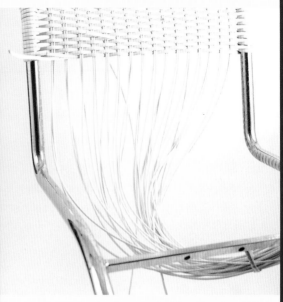

As you weave over and under a pair of spokes, put the spoke into the exact position you want it. The weavers will hold them in place. If you then pull the weavers too tight, you'll lose control of your spoke position. This is critical to holding the chair's shape.

For this type of project, you want the spokes to mimic the curve or shape of the chair. When you get to the middle curve of the chair, you don't want to pull the spokes and weavers too tight. You'll end up with a mound in the middle of the seat. It's very important that as you weave across, you adjust each spoke as the weaver passes it. You can't correct the shape later, but you do have absolute control of where the part of the spoke is at the moment you are weaving behind or in front of it.

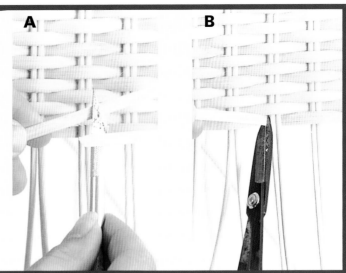

Finishing the Chair

STEP 1

As you weave down the back, make sure that the pairs of spokes remain parallel to each other and evenly spaced. Keep the weaving packed tightly together. When you finish weaving the chair, it will

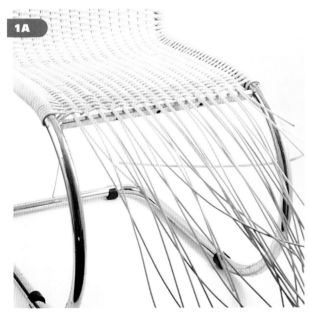

be time to anchor the spokes to the lower metal brace. Bring all the pairs of spokes on top of the lower metal brace (photo 1A).

Fit the second split rattan around the sides of the chair and on top and below the metal brace and under the pairs of spokes (photo 1B). Hold in position with the spring hand clamp.

STEP 2

Take a long length of ¼-inch (6 mm) flat oval reed (after soaking it in hot water for five minutes) and bend the last 2 inches (5 cm) into a right angle sideways to the strand (photo 2A). Lay the right-angle bend of the flat oval reed against the inside of the metal brace and wrap the flat oval reed around the split rattan and the metal brace, two times

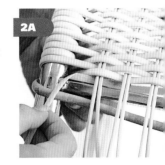

(photo 2B), keeping the wrap as close to the side of the chair as possible. Use the round-nose pliers to crimp the spoke to make a right-angle bend right at the inside edge of the metal brace.

STEP 3

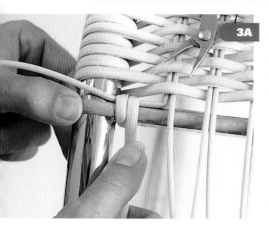

Carefully loosen the two wraps and slide the end of the spoke under the wrap and against the metal brace (photo 3A). You'll trim the end later. Tighten the wraps and continue wrapping around the spoke, the split rattan, and the metal brace. The pattern goes like this: three wraps around the spokes, then one wrap under the pair of spokes, then three wraps, then one, and so on, just like at the top of the chair.

STEP 4

When you get to the next pair of spokes, clamp the end of the wrapping strand to the leg of the chair, using the round-nose pliers to crimp both spokes where you want the bend. Trim the ends of the

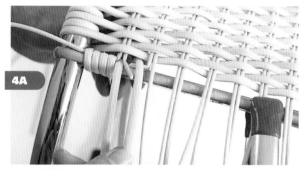

spokes so that they just fit in the space (photos 4A, 4B). You want them as long as possible so that three wraps will cover them, but you don't want them so long that they show or take over the adjacent space.

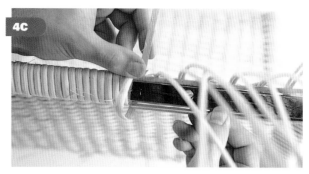

As you are crimping, cutting, and wrapping the ends of the spokes, keep in mind that you have to catch the other end of the split rattan (photo 4C). Keep the end of the split rattan clamped into position on the metal brace and, when you reach it, continue wrapping around it after removing the clamp.

STEP 5

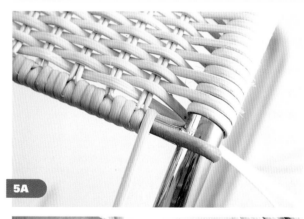

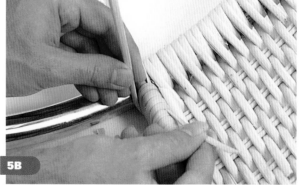

Crimp and trim the final spoke and wrap to the end of the brace. Turn the chair over and tuck the end of the wrapping strand back through the final two to three wraps and pull tight to secure the end (photos 5A, 5B).

Final Wrap

STEP 1

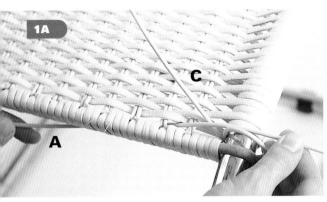

Begin the final three-rod twining (just like the top of the chair) by wrapping the middle of a long strand of #5 (3.25 mm) round reed twice around the side of the chair. One end of the round reed (C) will come up in the space between the side of the chair and the first pair of spokes. The other will go over the side of the chair and the first pair of spokes and then down in between the first and second pair of spokes (A) (photo 1A). Pull the round reed so that it is wrapped tightly around the side of the chair.

STEP 2

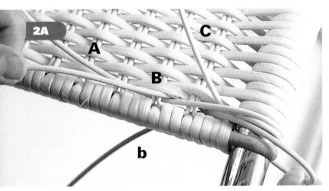

Bring the strand (A) up between the second and third pair of spokes. Insert another long strand of #5 (3.25 mm) round reed (B) down between the first and second pair of spokes and between the weaving of the seat and strand (A). Wrap the round reed around the side of the chair, then bring it down between the side of the chair and the first pair of spokes (b) (photo 2A). Leave this end of the

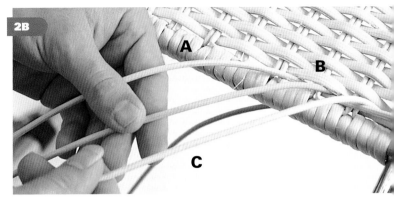

strand (b) in place. Do not use it in the three-strand twining. As you finish this step, check your results and make sure the three strands are in the right positions (photo 2B).

STEP 3

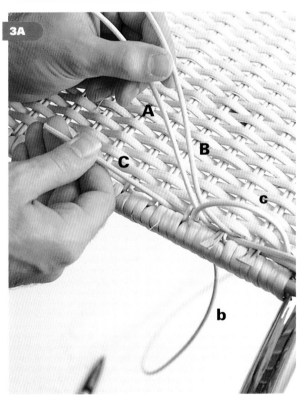

Bring strand C in front of strand B and strand A, insert between the second and third pair of spokes (marked with arrows), and bring it back out between the third and fourth pair of spokes (photo 3A). Continue the three-part twining as you did at the beginning of the chair.

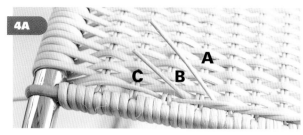

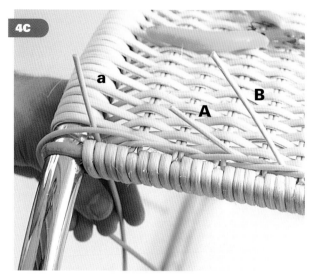

You may end up running out of reed before you reach the chair's side, just as it did in this example (photo 4A). Strand A stops four pairs of spokes short of the end of the row. Strand B stops three pairs of spokes short of the end of the row.

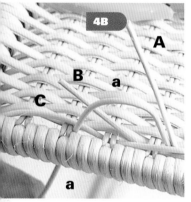

Insert a length of round reed (a) into the same space as strand A exits (photo 4B). Bring the other end of strand (a) over two pairs of spokes and down into the space between the second and third pair of strands from the end of the row. Then bring strand (a) up between the first and second pair of strands from the end of the row.

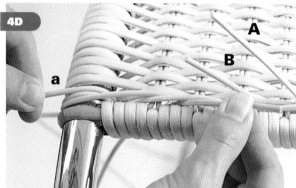

Bring strand (a) over the first pair of strands and the side of the chair two times. Then bring strand (a) up between the first and second pair of spokes (photos 4C, 4D). Take strand (a) over the second and third pair of spokes and insert it into the space next to strand B. Pull strand B back to make room

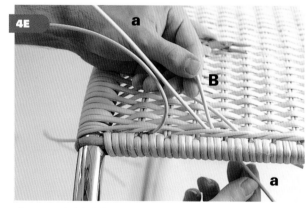

for strand (a) (photo 4E). Pull strand (a) down and tight. Trim all the ends close but still past the spoke they pass behind to keep them locked into position.

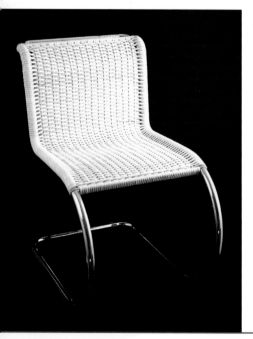

Modern Elegance.
The finished Mies Van Der Rohe chair

UNDO THE DAMAGE OF TIME AND USE: REPAIRS TO WICKER FURNITURE

Many repairs to wicker furniture can be made without reweaving the entire piece from scratch. That's the case in this next example where the chair arm has been crushed.

Tools and Materials

1 coil of #5 (3.25 mm) round reed
Needle-nose pliers

STEP 1

To repair this broken arm, the supporting spokes—which help define the shape of the arm—and a number of weavers will need to be replaced. Notice the broken spokes below the arm that attach to the seat frame (photo 1A).

To start, new spokes are inserted from the inside of the arm (photo 1B). Use the needle-nose pliers to pull the spokes through the weave, a few weavers at a time. Use one hand with the pliers to pull, the other hand below helps push the spoke through the weave (photo 1C). Bring the spoke all the way through the weave (photo 1D). Duplicate this step as needed until all the broken spokes are replaced. Make sure you have enough

length pulled through the weave to finish the spokes in a border (photo 1E).

STEP 2

Use the needle-nose pliers to kink the spoke where it will make a 90° bend for the border (photo 2A). The other end of the spokes will be anchored to the seat frame with staples.

Good as new. The completed repair to this wicker seat's arm, ready for painting

Repairing a Ball Foot

The ball foot, a frequently seen feature in wicker furniture, is woven in a similar manner to the Wheat Straw corn dollie spiral, but instead of each spoke interacting with the adjacent spoke, the transitioning spoke goes under the adjacent spoke to interact with the second spoke. In order for this process to work, you need an odd number of spokes.

In our example, the form for the ball was a shaped piece of wood with the center drilled out so that it would slide over the end of the leg. Nine holes are evenly spaced around the ball and drilled into the end of the ball. The angle of the drill also grooved the leg where the ball was held. There are no nails holding the ball in place. The thickness of the spoke material, and the fact that the spokes also lie in these grooves in the leg, keep the ball in place.

I have also seen a ball formed by several layers of round reed or fiber rush wrapped around the end of the leg to make the ball shape over which the weave is created.

While the ball foot can be woven from round reed, typically it was woven from seagrass cordage or later, fiber rush.

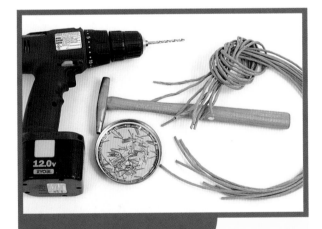

Tools and Materials

9 strands of ⅛-inch (3 mm) Kraft Brown
   Fiber Rush, 36 inches (92 cm) long each
Drill with ⅛-inch (3 mm) drill bit
½-inch (1.3 cm) x 20-gauge wire nails
Tack hammer

In the example used here (left), nine holes have been drilled around the end of the wood form. If the ball you're working on is made from reed or cordage, the ends of the nine spokes can be nailed to the end of the leg and the form then wound around the ends.

down second spoke and behind the next spoke to the left (photo 1C).

STEP 1

Insert one strand of fiber rush into each hole. For the first row only, a spoke is taken directly behind the adjacent spoke to the left (photo 1A). Take the adjacent spoke to the left, over the turned down first spoke, and behind the next spoke to the left (photo 1B). Take that third spoke over the turned-

STEP 2

Continue all the way around the leg. As you do, notice how the last spoke (B) is still sticking up (photo 2A). Take (B) over the most recently turned-down spoke (A), under the first turned-down spoke (C) and up. Twist (C) and (B) so that they change positions (photo 2B).

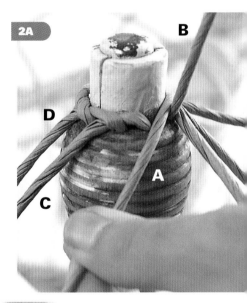

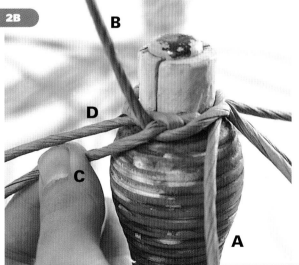

STEP 3

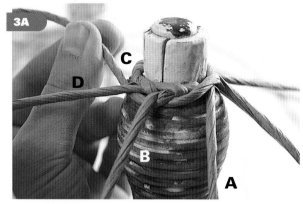

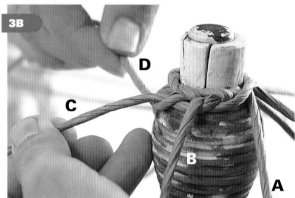

Bring the new spoke (C) under the adjacent spoke (D) and up and twist (photo 3A). Drop the spoke (C) and pick up the next spoke (D) (photo 3B). This spoke will now be the transitioning member. Bring the spoke (D) under the adjacent spoke and up and twist. Then drop this spoke, pick up the spoke that was just passed over, and continue the pattern with the new member.

STEP 4

Continue the pattern around the ball. For the next and the succeeding rows, bring the transitioning spoke under two spokes and make the twist with the second spoke. Pick up that second spoke, go under the next two spokes, and make the twist with the second spoke (photo 4A). Continue around the foot

many more times until you reach the bottom of the foot (photo 4B).

STEP 5

When you have reached the bottom of the ball foot, choose the longest spoke that is left and use it to wind around the other spokes to hold them together (photo 5A). Use a ½-inch (1.3 cm), 20-gauge wire nail to tack the winding strand in place. If you plan to paint or stain the repair, seal the fiber rush or seagrass with primer or clear sealer, then paint or stain as usual.

All tied up.
The completed repairs to a classic chair's ball foot

Once the rattan arrives at the furniture factory, the canes are sorted by diameter. Because of the over-harvesting of wild rattans, there is very little found today that is over 2 inches (5 cm) in diameter.

The next step determines which canes are of the quality necessary to make chair cane. The distance between the nodes must be as long as possible, and they must be very smooth. The nodes aren't actually growth nodes as in bamboo, but are attachment points for the leaves and thorns. The bark or peel of these canes must be strong and mostly unaffected by the removal of the leaves and thorns.

Once these canes are selected, they're put through a machine that removes the peel in strips and leaves a smooth pole of inner core of rattan. The rattan core is put through other machines to make different sizes of round reed, split round reed, flat reed, flat-oval reed, oval reed, and spline. The strips of rattan peel are put through thinning and trimming machines to make the 12 different sizes of chair cane and binder cane.

The peel is bundled into 1,000-foot (303 m) hanks, folded in half, and tied securely. Unless the client has requested long select strands, these hanks will also contain random length strands ranging from 6 to 20 feet (1.8 to 6 m) each. A hank of chair cane is 1,000 linear feet (303 m) and if it contains all long strands, there will be fewer strands in the hank than a 1,000-foot (303 m) hank of random length strands. A quick check of the number of strands at the fold reveals whether or not the hank contains many long strands.

Once thinned, trimmed, and sorted, reeds are bundled into one pound hanks and then fashioned into hanks or coils as needed by the customer.

Left: Machine trimming of chair cane to precise size. *Below:* Glueing thinned ends of chair cane together to make an endless strand for loomed cane.
PHOTOS BY DENNIS LEE

Gallery

Restored seagrass armchair

Restored child's seagrass rocker after staining

Top: Child's seagrass rocker before restoration

Bottom: Detail of rattan arm structure in child's seagrass rocker before restoration

Child's seagrass rocker after restoration

CHAPTER 6

Tie It All Together: Rattan Repairs and Decorative Wraps

Do you have rattan furniture with frayed and cracked wraps you'd like to repair? Then this is the chapter for you. You'll be introduced to ways of using rattan to decorate common household items as well as many ways of replacing all those unsightly broken and worn out join wraps on your rattan tables and chairs. Once you see how easy it is to do, you'll probably come up with a few wrapping styles of your own.

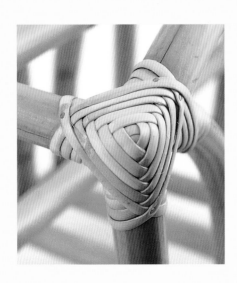

DECORATIVE RATTAN WRAPS

Binder cane (wide chair cane) is the material usually used for making decorative and structural wraps on rattan and bamboo furniture. When binder cane is soaked in hot water for five to 10 minutes, it becomes pliable and stretches a bit. As it dries, it shrinks and makes a very tight join. Glue and nails are rarely necessary with rattan wraps and joins.

Tools and Materials

6 mm binder cane

The Basic Wrap

STEP 1

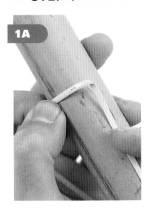

Soak a length of binder cane in hot water for five minutes. Take the length of binder cane and fold the first couple of inches (5 cm) at a right-angle. The bark side of the end of the strand will lie against the leg to be wrapped (photo 1A).

STEP 2

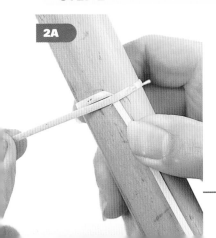

Wind the strand around the leg and the end of the strand that is flat against the leg (photo 2A). When you are ready to end the wrap, make another

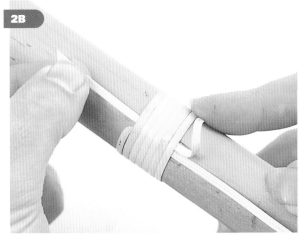

right-angle fold with the end of the strand and run it under the wraps you have completed. You will need to loosen the wraps slightly in order to insert the end of the strand (photo 2B). After the strand is inserted through the wrap, tighten the wraps and

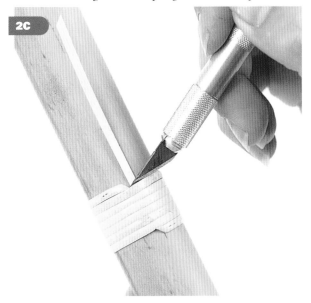

pull the strand taut. Trim the ends of the strand so that they are hidden under the wrap (photo 2C).

Joining a New Strand in the Basic Wrap

STEP 1

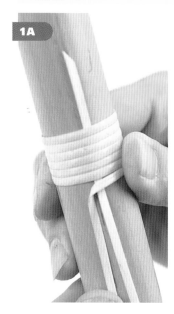

Begin the wrap as in the previous exercise. Insert the new strand under the wrap. Make a right-angle fold with the end of the original wrap so that the end is just past and parallel to the new strand. The bark side of the binder cane (both pieces) is against the leg (photo 1A).

STEP 2

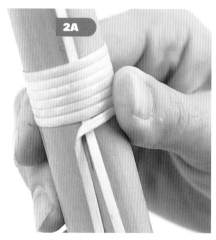

Make a right-angle fold with the new piece of binder cane (photo 2A) so that the fold fits into the fold of the original length of cane, and continue wrapping. Notice that the join virtually disappears as it becomes a part of the wrap (photo 2B).

A Decorative Wrapping Pattern

STEP 1

Begin the wrap as before. After wrapping about 1 inch (2.5 cm) or more, insert five strands of binder cane—each about 8 inches (20.3 cm) long—under the wrap so the strands lie next to each and perpendicular to the wrap (photo 1A). Bring the wrap over the first two short strands, under the middle strand, and then over the last two short strands (photo 1B). Repeat this step.

STEP 2

On the next circuit, bring the wrap over the first short strand, under the three middle strands, and over the last short strand (photo 2A). Repeat this step. On the next circuit, bring the wrap under all five short strands. Do not repeat this step.

STEP 3

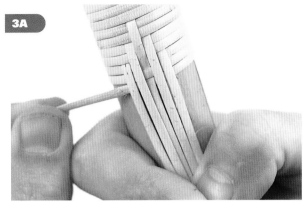

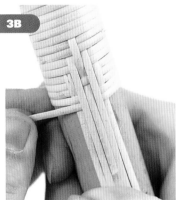

On the next wrap, bring the strand under the first two short strands, over the middle strand, then over the last two short strands. Do not repeat this step. You'll then bring the wrap under all five short strands (photo 3A). Do not repeat this step. Continue by bringing the wrap over the first short strand, under the middle three strands, and over the last short strand (photo 3B). Repeat this step.

STEP 4

With the next circuit, bring the wrap over the first two short strands, under the middle strand, and over

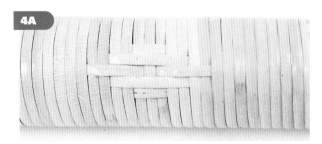

the last two short strands. Repeat this step. On the last circuit, bring the wrap over all five short strands. Repeat this step (photo 4A).

A Decorative Knot

This decorative knot is an elegant addition to a teapot or basket handle. It can also be used to hide a four-way crossing on a piece of furniture.

STEP 1

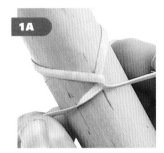

Soak a length of binder cane in hot water for five minutes. Make a loop at the end of the piece of binder cane. Bring the other end around and through the loop (photo 1A).

STEP 2

After passing through the loop, reverse the direction and bring the end around and up through the loop on the other side (photo 2A).

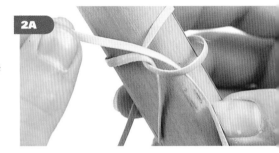

STEP 3

Pull the wrap tight (photo 3A). Follow the strand around and repeat the same process of going around, pass through the loop and reverse direction (photo 3B).

STEP 4

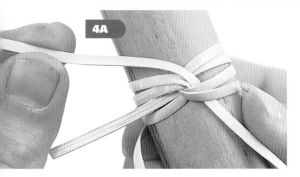

Pull the wrap tight. Continue these steps until you have gone around four or five times (photo 4A).

STEP 5

When finished, both ends may be trimmed (photo 5A). A drop of glue may be used if needed.

The Decorative Knot with an Addition

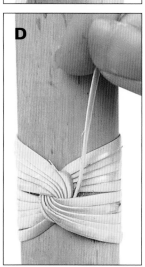

Instead of cutting the end after the previous step, bring the end of the strand up over the wraps to the 2:00 position, then under the wraps toward the 8:00 position (photos A, B), through the wraps back to the 2:00 position (photo C), and then under the wraps back towards the 8:00 position. Continue this wheel pattern four or five times (photo D), then trim the end. A drop of glue will ensure the knot won't unravel.

WRAPPING A TEAPOT HANDLE

Embellishing items with rattan can add a certain flair and distinctiveness to them, as well as improve functionality. Take a look at the creative way a teapot handle can be made safer and a decorative focal point at the same time.

Tools and Materials

1 to 3 lengths of 4 mm binder cane

STEP 1

Make a 90° fold with the end of a length of cane (photo 1A). The bark side of the cane should be against the handle. Bring the end of the cane around the teapot handle and the fold. Continue wrapping neatly around the handle.

STEP 2

After five wraps, insert two lengths of cane into the wrap (photo 2A). Wrap twice under the two lengths of cane (photo 2B), then twice over the two

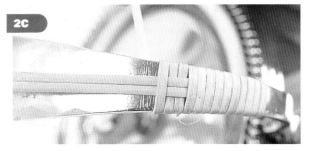

lengths of cane (photo 2C). Continue the wrapping pattern of two over and two under until you reach the other side of the handle. Tuck the end of the

wrapping strand under the last three wraps, tighten the wraps, and pull the end snug (photo 2D). Trim the end. A tiny drop of instant bonding glue can be used, but should not be necessary (photo 2E).

WRAPS FOR REPAIRING RATTAN AND BAMBOO FURNITURE

In the following examples, you'll learn some rattan first-aid techniques you can use for just about any piece of rattan furniture. Using this vintage magazine rack (right) will show you a number of different types of commonly used joins.

If you wish to get even more involved in the art of crafting rattan furniture from scratch, you can find complete instructions listed on the author's website (see page 119). In the meantime, here's a partial list of what you might need to repair a typical piece of rattan furniture:

Bent on learning. This vintage magazine rack, with all its varying joins and bends, makes an excellent subject for learning new styles of rattan wraps.

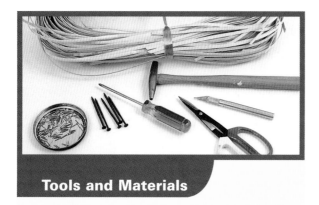

Tools and Materials

1 hank of 6 mm wide binder cane
Nails or coarse threaded screws
   2½-inches (6.4 cm) long
Screwdriver
Shears
½-inch (1.3 cm) x 20-gauge wire nails

Three-Part Corner Join (with additional brace)

You can use this type of wrap when you need to cover the intersection of two horizontal members meeting level with the top of a leg (an extra leg brace joins diagonally just below the intersection in this example).

If nailed structural pieces are loose, remove the nails and use screws to secure the pieces together. The wraps will cover the nail or screw heads.

STEP 1

Take a long strand of binder cane (matching the width of that used on the rest of the piece—usually 5mm or 6mm binder cane) and soak it in hot water for 5 minutes. Lay the strand across the top of the leg and let 3 inches (7.6 cm) hang over the front corner of the leg. Set a ½-inch (1.3 cm) x 20-gauge wire nail through the cane into the front corner of the leg. Trim the end of the cane within ½ inch (1.3 cm) of the nail head (photo 1A).

STEP 2

Wind the strand behind and around the side rung to the left of the corner and over the top of the leg post (photo 2A), then

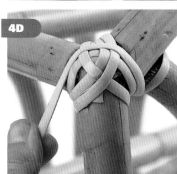

below and up behind the side rung to the right of the corner (photo 2B). Bring the cane over the top of the leg post and below the top corner of the leg post so that it catches on the corner (photo 2C).

STEP 3

Take the strand back under the side rung to the left of the corner post (photo 3A).

Bring it up and over the top of the corner post—slightly to the left of the previous crossing—and go around the corner post to the right (photo 3B). Come behind the corner post below the side rungs (photo 3C), and cross up to the right side of the corner post and slightly below and to the right of the previous crossing (photo 3D).

STEP 4

Take the cane behind the side rung to the right of the corner post and to the left of the curved support piece that is to the right of the corner post. Then bring the cane up and completely around the curved support piece (photos 4A, 4B, 4C). Continue by taking the cane completely over the corner post to the right of the center of the forming decorative knot (photo 4D), then around from behind the left side rung (photo 4E).

STEP 5

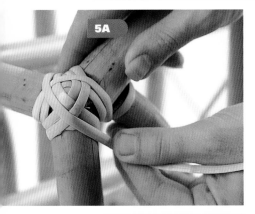

Next, bring the cane around and below the corner post, keeping the strand slightly below the last crossing (photo 5A). Bring it back around the leg post and up toward the right side rung. Wrap around the right side rung keeping the cane to the right of the previous crossing (photos 5B, 5C). Bring the cane out between the right side rung and around the lower curved support piece (photo 5D).

STEP 6

Wrap the strand up and to the left over the top of the corner leg post and toward the front of the left side support. Then guide the strand around the left side support and across the top of the corner post, keeping the strand to the left of the previous crossing (photos 6A, 6B). Bring the cane around the leg, cross up to the right and put a ½-inch (1.3 cm), 20-gauge wire nail through the two strands at the crossing to keep them from shifting (photo 6C).

STEP 7

Following the previous pattern, bring the cane up and over the corner and tuck the end of the strand under the previous row (photo 7A). Pull the strand tight and use a ½-inch 20-gauge wire nail through the two strands to anchor the end of the cane. Use a sharp knife to trim the end of the cane so that it is hidden (photo 7B).

Four Way T-Join

Use this style of wrap to hide a join like the one in our magazine rack example where the handle and short side support come together. The handle is notched to accommodate the side support to keep the handle from shifting.

STEP 1

Use a ½-inch, 20-gauge wire nail to attach the last 2 to 3 inches (5 to 7.6 cm) of cane to the side of the handle. Trim the end of the cane to within ½ inch (1.3 cm) of the nail head.

STEP 2

Bring the cane around behind the handle to the left side of the handle (photo 2A), then behind the handle and across to the right side (photo 2B).

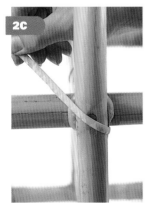

Now take the cane around and up across the handle (photo 2C), straight around the handle, then across from the upper right to the lower left across the

handle (photo 2D). The cane then passes straight across behind the handle, then crosses up from the lower right to the upper left, just above the previous crossing, then straight across behind the handle, then crosses down from the upper right to the lower left, just above the previous crossing (photo 2E).

STEP 3

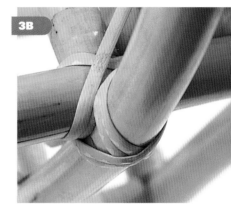

Bring the cane around behind the handle and up against the side rung (photo 3A), then across the side rung, behind the handle in a half 'X', and then around the side rung (photo 3B). Finish the 'X',

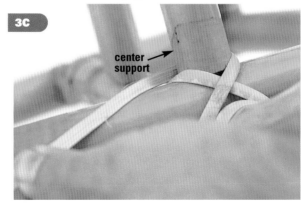

center support

and wrap the cane around the center support (photo 3C).

STEP 4

Wrap the cane around the center support piece three times, tuck the end of the strand back under the final wrap, pull tight and use a ½-inch (1.3 cm), 20-gauge wire nail to secure the end of the wrap (photos 4A, 4B).

Traditional T-Join

Use this technique to hide a butt-join that comes together in a *T*.

STEP 1

Anchor the end of a strand at the butt-join of the two pieces of rattan. Use a ½-inch (1.3 cm), 20-gauge wire nail (photo 1A). Wrap the cane one time completely around the butted end section. Bring the cane at an angle around the longer section of rattan (photo 1B).

STEP 2

Guide the strand straight around the longer section, then at an angle back to the left side of the butted section (photo 2A). Now wrap the strand completely around the butted end section, then bring the strand up at an angle and to the right of the previous crossing (photo 2B).

STEP 3

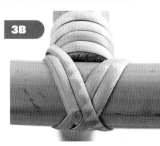

Bring the strand straight down behind the longer rattan section and up at an angle to the left side of the butted end section, keeping the strand to the right of the previous crossing (photo 3A). Wrap it completely around the shorter butted end section, then tuck the end under the final wrap and anchor the end of the strand with a ½-inch (1.3 cm), 20-gauge wire nail (photo 3B).

Two Horizontals Meet a Leg at the Same Level

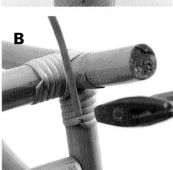

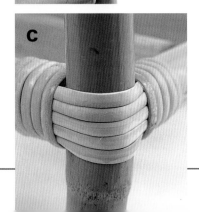

Anchor five horizontal strands of 6 mm binder cane around and over the join (photo A). A single strand of 6 mm binder cane then wraps around both side supports (photo B). The end of the strand is anchored with a ½-inch (1.3 cm), 20-gauge wire nail through two layers of cane to finish off the wrap (photo C).

SPLITTING RATTAN

Learning to split rattan by hand is easy. It just takes practice. Go slowly. You can actually steer the split back and forth by pulling harder on one side. You want to pull as evenly as possible to keep the split down the center of the stick. Once you learn this technique, you'll find you can split many other caning materials including white oak, thin willow sticks, and thinner rattans as well.

the split (photo 2B). Your thumbs will help control the split in this position. Pull the split apart, slowly, with your hands.

STEP 1

First, place a sharp knife, edge down, across the middle of the end of a rattan stick. Push the blade into the cross section (photo 1A). Using a hammer or small mallet, tap the blade down into the stick so that it begins to split the rattan stick (photo 1B).

STEP 3

If the split starts to move to one side, pull down harder on the *thicker* side to make the split move back toward center (photo 3A). If you go too fast, the split can quickly work its way past the middle, in which case you'll have to pull down harder with the other hand to get the split back into the middle.

STEP 2

Twist the blade of the knife sideways to widen the split—this will also cause the split to continue down the stick (photo 2A). When the split is wide enough so that you can grab both sides of the split with your hands, position your hands with your thumbs up and against the outer sides of

Scraping Rattan Nodes

Use a sharp knife to carefully trim any leaf remnants from the rattan nodes. Remove as little of the silica bark as possible. The node should make a smooth transition so that anyone running his hand across the rattan will only feel a smooth surface (bottom, right).

The Rattan Road
The Future of the Rattan Industry and Trade

Of the 600 species of rattan found in the rain forests of Southeast Asia, only a few dozen are actually useful to the furniture industry. The problem is that it's hard to know which species is which. Until the 1960s, furniture makers could be reasonably sure harvesters were careful in selecting rattan because of an abundant supply. Today, once the supply of a preferred species is exhausted, it's no longer feasible to move on to another area to locate it. The area might not be accessible from the harvester's village, or the price for the rattan is not worth extended exploration.

Realizing that the most desirable species of rattan were becoming harder to find, leaders in industry, government, and botany formed the Rattan Information Center. Over the next 10 years, surveys were taken of the rattan species of the Southeast Asian countries, and studies were undertaken to determine why one species was preferable to another. Many small rattan farms were begun in association with rubber trees and oil palms to see if forest conditions could be simulat-

A closer look at the thorny exterior of a rattan vine shows why harvesting it can be a dicey proposition. Photo courtesy of David Hall, Haas School of Business, University of California Berkeley, and the P3R Organization, Kalimantan, Indonesia

ed for the rattans. However, the larger rattans still need the natural forests.

If use of rattan without regard for regeneration continues at the current rate, our rattan reserves will be exhausted. If we're going to continue to have a rattan resource, we must encourage Southeast Asian governments to slow down or cease the destruction of their rain forest habitats and look to better utilizing their resource on a long-term basis.

We must also encourage consumers to choose certified, sustainable harvested rattan supplies. Forest certification practices promote better forest stewardship, ensure environmental responsibility, and cause socially beneficial and economically viable management of forests to be put into practice. These policies help protect our natural resources, which help to ensure a healthy planet.

A local worker shown wrestling vines from other surrounding jungle growth. PHOTO BY STEPHEN SIEBERT

Gallery

Ceramic teapot with rattan handle

Rattan tub chair after minor restoration

Re-caned McGuire Campaign Chair with rawhide wraps

Gallery

Finished Cross X wrap

Rawhide leg brace wrap on
McGuire Campaign Chair

Variations in join wraps

APPENDIX A
STYLES OF NATURAL PRE-WOVEN CANE WEBBING

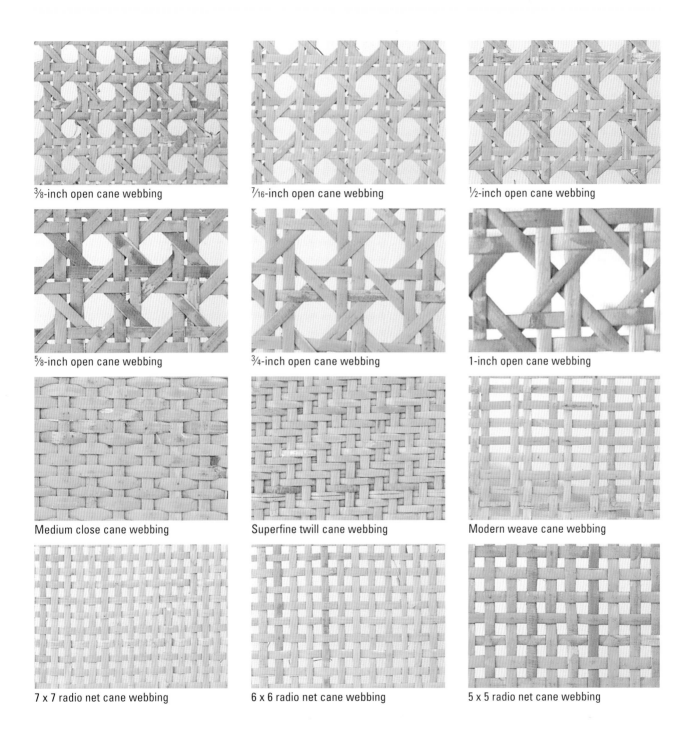

3/8-inch open cane webbing

7/16-inch open cane webbing

1/2-inch open cane webbing

5/8-inch open cane webbing

3/4-inch open cane webbing

1-inch open cane webbing

Medium close cane webbing

Superfine twill cane webbing

Modern weave cane webbing

7 x 7 radio net cane webbing

6 x 6 radio net cane webbing

5 x 5 radio net cane webbing

APPENDIX B
DIAMOND PATTERN WEAVING CHART

			X	X	X											X	X	X					X	X	X					X	X
		X	X	X										X	X	X						X	X	X					X	X	
	X	X	X						X	X	X				X	X	X					X	X	X				X	X	X	
X	X	X				X	X	X				X	X	X					X	X	X		X	X	X				X	X	X
X	X				X	X	X					X	X	X	X	X					X	X	X							X	X
X			X	X	X					X	X	X				X	X	X				X	X	X							X
		X	X	X				X	X	X				X	X	X					X	X	X					X	X	X	
	X	X	X				X	X	X				X	X	X					X	X	X					X	X	X		
X	X	X				X	X	X				X	X	X					X	X	X				X	X	X				
X	X	X			X	X	X				X	X	X	X	X				X	X	X					X	X	X			
X	X			X	X	X				X	X	X	X	X	X					X	X	X							X	X	
X			X	X	X				X	X	X		X	X	X				X	X	X					X	X	X			X
		X	X	X			X	X	X			X	X	X				X	X	X					X	X	X				X
X			X	X	X			X	X	X			X	X	X				X	X	X										X
X	X			X	X	X			X	X	X	X	X					X	X	X					X	X	X			X	X
X	X	X			X	X	X			X	X	X				X	X	X					X	X	X				X	X	X
	X	X	X			X	X	X				X				X	X	X				X	X	X				X	X	X	
		X	X	X			X	X	X						X	X	X				X	X	X				X	X	X		
		X	X	X			X	X	X			X	X	X				X	X	X				X	X	X					
X			X	X	X			X	X	X		X	X	X				X	X	X					X	X	X				X
X	X			X	X	X			X	X	X	X	X					X	X	X					X	X	X			X	X
X	X	X			X	X	X			X	X	X				X	X	X					X	X	X				X	X	X
	X	X	X			X	X	X				X				X	X	X				X	X	X				X	X	X	
		X	X	X			X	X	X						X	X	X				X	X	X				X	X	X		
		X	X	X			X	X	X			X	X	X				X	X	X				X	X	X					

Epilogue

In the 20th century, a number of architects and furniture designers (Mies Van Der Rohe, Marcel Breuer, and Hans Wegner) built sturdy, lightweight, comfortable furniture of wood, steel, and cane that continues to appreciate in value today. Their designs are enduring, and their materials are easily reparable and available. Undoubtedly, the 21st century will see new, synthetic discoveries being used to create imaginative, enduring chair frames in need of comfortable seating material. All that is needed is a willing caner to tackle the new challenge.

Author Information

Jim Widess has owned The Caning Shop in Berkeley, California, since 1971. He is the co-author and photographer of *The Caner's Handbook* (Lark Books, 1991), *The Complete Book of Gourd Craft* (Lark Books, 1996), *Making Gourd Musical Instruments* (Sterling Publishing, 1999), *Making Hawaiian Ribbon Leis* (Mutual Publishing, 2002), and *Complete Book of Gourd Carving* (Sterling Publishing, 2004). He is also the author and photographer of *Making Hawaiian Musical Instruments* (Mutual Publishing, 2002) and *Gourd Pyrography* (Sterling Publishing, 2002). Jim has a zeal for visual instructions for crafts.

Questions for the author may be sent to jimwidess@caning.com
Please visit the author's web site at http://www.caning.com

GLOSSARY

Ash. Ash is pounded so that the wood separates naturally at its growth rings. Long, flat weaving material is easily produced. Very strong and long-lasting splints.

Binder Cane. Chair cane that is wider than 3.5 mm; narrow binder is 4 mm wide; medium binder is 5 mm wide; wide binder is 6 mm wide; extra-wide binder is 7 to 8 mm wide; shaved slab is 8 to 10 mm wide.

Blind Cane. A hand cane panel in which the holes do not go all the way through the wood. Each individual strand is cut and pegged into the hole. There are no loops connecting the strands. Frequently found on backs of chairs. Not recommended for seats. French caned panels are usually blind caned.

Braided Seagrass. Chinese seagrass that has been pre-braided. Used in some vintage seagrass chairs.

Bulrush. Scirpus; Either round or triangular cross section.

Cane. Rattan peel cut into thin strips of different widths for weaving cane seats.

Cane Webbing. Loom-woven chair cane for seats.

Cattails. Flat leaves used to weave rush seats in the United States.

Center Cane. A United Kingdom term for the pithy rattan core. Distinguishes round reed from willow.

Danish Cord. A very high-quality paper cord manufactured in Denmark. Two styles: laced and unlaced. The laced has a more rope-like quality because both plies are twisted as they are twisted together. The unlaced has a smoother feel because the individual plies are left untwisted as the twine is manufactured.

Datu. Light tan color, 2.5 to 4.5 mm diameter whole rattan.

Double Cane. Same as French cane.

Fiber Rush. A one-ply, twisted paper product made to imitate natural rush.

Flat Oval Reed. Rattan core cut into strips that are flat on one side and rounded on the other.

Flat Reed. Rattan core cut into strips that are flat on both sides.

French Cane. Refers to a piece of furniture that has a double hand caned panel, i.e. there is caning on both sides of the panel as in a chair back or footboard for a bed.

Gusset. The triangular space on either side of a splint or rush seat formed when the front rail is longer than the back rail.

Hand Cane. Weaving the traditional octagonal pattern strand for strand by hand.

Hickory Bark. The two layers of wood that lie on either side of the cambium layer of the hickory tree after scraping off the rough outer bark of the tree itself.

Hong Kong Grass. Same as seagrass.

Kooboo. Light tan color, 6 to 15 mm diameter whole rattan.

Manau. Large diameter 15 to 45 mm. Whole rattan. Longer distance between nodes. Most desirable species of furniture rattan.

Natural Rush. In Europe, bulrush (a round sedge). In the United States, rush usually refers to cattails (a flat leaf).

Oak. Quercus; White oak is easily split along its growth rings so that flat weaving material is easily produced.

Paper Cane. A resin-impregnated, reinforced woven paper product that some furniture manufacturers use instead of woven natural cane, for chair backs and large decorative furniture applications. Available in many patterns. Not recommended for seats.

Paper Rush. See Fiber Rush.

Prairie Grass. Carex stricta; Tough, fibrous pest that grew in Minnesota and Wisconsin. Made popular at the turn of the century by the American Grass Twine Company as a substitute for rattan or willow. Remained popular until the close of World War I. Difficult to distinguish furniture made from prairie grass and seagrass.

Pre-twisted Natural Rush. A newer product from China made from seagrass that has been twisted into a one-ply cord meant to imitate natural rush. A stiffer material than fiber rush.

Pre-woven Cane. Another name for cane webbing.

Puloet. 4 to 6 mm diameter whole rattan. Slightly reddish color.

Raffia. From Madagascar and the Philippines. It is the leaf of the raffia palm that has been split and the outer layer of the leaf removed, leaving the fibrous, strong, inner layer.

Rattan. One of some 600 species and 6 genera of palms that grow like a vine in the rain forests of Southeast Asia and Africa. Also refers to furniture made from rattan palms.

Rattan Core. The material left over after the rattan skin is removed from the rattan stem.

Rattan Peel. The inner skin cut from the rattan stem.

Rawhide. Animal hide, usually cow, that is stretched, and dried. Cut into strips and used for wrapping joins on rattan furniture made by the McGuire Company. The McGuire Company has a patent on this process.

Round Reed. Rattan core cut into round strips of different diameters.

Rush. Refers to the chair seat weaving pattern which uses a one-ply, twisted "rush" (cattails, bulrush, paper fiber) to weave a pattern which results usually in four triangles that meet in the center of the seat.

Seagrass. A thin rush which grows in salt water tidal areas in China.

Setting. European terms for the courses in hand caning. The first setting would be steps one and three; the second setting would be steps two and four.

Shaker Tape. A flat, woven fabric, ⅝ to 2 inches wide, use to weave seats and backs of ladder back chairs and stools in the Shaker communities of the East coast of the United States.

Sheet Cane. Another name for cane webbing.

Splint. Flat material such as white oak or hickory bark, used in weaving seats on chairs with round rails.

Split Round Reed. Rattan core cut into strips that are shaped like half-round reed.

Untwisted Seagrass. Individual stems of Chinese seagrass, ideal for braiding and twining or making cordage.

Wicker. The weaving process of over-and under spoke warps. May be woven from any round or flat material. Refers to the weave, not the material.

Willow. Long flexible one-year shoots of the Salix genus. Used for weaving baskets, chests, and furniture, often in a wicker weave.

Warp. The loom threads through which the "weft" strands will be woven.

BIBLIOGRAPHY

Adamson, Jeremy, *American Wicker: Woven Furniture from 1850 to 1930,* Rizzoli, NY, 1993

Alth, Max and Charlotte, *How to Make Your Own Cane Furniture,* Hawthorn Books, NY, 1979

Archaeological Institute of the Chinese Academy of Sciences, "Report on the Excavations at Huixian County," Science Press, Beijing, 1956.

Bahadur, Mutua, *Cane and Bamboo Crafts of Manipur,* Mutua Museum, New Delhi, 1994

Bishop, Robert, *Centuries and Styles of the American Chair 1640–1970,* E. P. Dutton, NY, 1972

Broan, David and **Freda,** *Cane and Rush Seating: A Practical Guide,* Bishopgate Press Ltd., London, 1981

Burkill, L. H., *A Dictionary of Economic Products of the Malay Peninsula,* 2 Volumes, London, 1935

Canter-Visscher, Estelle, *Working with Cane,* Wilson & Hobert Ltd, Auckland, 1984

Corbin, Patricia, *All About Wicker,* E. P. Dutton, NY, 1978

Corner, E., *The Natural History of Palms,* UC Press, Berkeley, 1966

Crossman, Carl L., *The China Trade – Export Paintings, Furniture, Silver and Other Objects,* Pyne Press, Princeton, 1972.

Duncan, Thomas, *How to Buy and Restore Wicker Furniture,* Sylvan Books, MI, 1983

Ecke, Gustav, *Chinese Domestic Furniture,* Chas. Tuttle, 1962

Ellsworth, Robert H., *Chinese Hardwood Furniture in Hawaiian Collections,* Honolulu Academy of Arts, Honolulu, 1982

Ellsworth, Robert H., *Chinese Furniture— Hardwood Examples of the Ming and Early Ch'ing Dynasties,* New Fairfield, CT, 1997

Emberlein, Harold Donaldson; and **Ramsdell, Roger Wearne**, *The Practical Book of Italian, Spanish and Portuguese Furniture,* J.B. Lippincott Company, Philadelphia, 1927

Forman, Benno, *American Seating Furniture – 1630-1730 An Interpretive Catalogue.* Winterthur Book, W. W. Norton, 1988

Franks, Beth, *Wicker, Cane, and Willow,* Grove-Weidenfeld, NY, 1990

Greenwood, Levi H., *A Completed Century 1826-1926, The Story of Heywood-Wakefield Company,* Boston, 1926

Guerin, Denis, *Cannez Rempaillez vous Chaises, Dessain et Tolra,* Paris, 2001

Gurrl, Kim; Straker, Leon; and Moore, Phillip, *A History of Seating in the Western World,* Curtin University of Technology, Perth, Western Australia. Online publication

Handler, Sarah, *Austere Luminosity of Chinese Classical Furniture,* University of California Press, Berkeley, 2001

Handler, Sarah, "The Ubiquitous Stool," Journal of the Classical Chinese Furniture Society, Summer, 1994, pp. 4-23

Herrick, Wm. D., *History of the Town of Gardner, Worcester County, Massachusets,* The Committee, 1879

Heywood-Wakefield, *Antique Wicker,* 1929 catalog reprint, Schiffer, PA 1994

Hill, Conover, *Antique Wicker Furniture,* Collector Books, KY 1975

Holdstock, Ricky, *Seat Weaving, Guild of Master Craftsman Publications,* London, 1989

Hurd, D. Hamilton, *History of Worcester County Massachusets,* J. W. Lewis, 1889

Jaffer, Amin, *Furniture from British India and Ceylon,* V&A Publications, London, 2001

Johnson, Kay; Barratt, Olivia Elton; and **Butcher, Mary,** *Chair Seating Techniques in Cane, Rush, Willow, and Cords,* Dryad Press, London, 1988

Kates, George N., *Chinese Household Furniture,* Dover Publications, NY, 1962

Killen, Geoffrey, *Ancient Egyptian Furniture, Vol. 1,* Aris and Phillips Ltd, Warminster Wiltshire, 1980

Killen, Geoffrey, *Egyptian Woodworking and Furniture,* Shire Publication, London, 1994

Kuhn, Dieter, *Chinese Baskets and Mats,* Franz Steiner Publishers, Wiesbaden, 1980

Malekandathil, Pius, *Portuguese Cochin and the Maritime Trade of India 1500-1663,* Manohar, New Delhi, 2001

Meng, Ho Wing, *Straits Chinese Furniture—A Collector's Guide,* Times Editions Pte Ltd, Singapore, 1994

Miller, Bruce; and **Widess, Jim,** *The Caner's Handbook,* Van Nostrand Reinhold, NY, 1983

Morse, Frances Clary, *Furniture of the Olden Time,* Macmillan Company, NY, 1937

Nicholson, Paul and **Ian Shaw,** *Ancient Egyptian Materials and Technology,* Cambridge University Press, Cambridge 2001

Perry, L. Day, *Seat Weaving: A Manual for Furniture Fixers,* Chas Scribner's Sons, NY, 1917

Piper, Jacqueline M., *Bamboo and Rattan Traditional Uses and Beliefs,* Oxford University Press, Singapore, 1992

Ranjan, M.P., *Bamboo and Cane Crafts of Northeast India,* National Institute of Design, New Delhi, 1986

Rees, Yvonne, *Caning and Rushwork,* Wardlock, London, 1993

Richter, G.M., *Furniture of the Greeks, Etruscans, and Romans,* Phaidan Press, London, 1966

Saunders, Richard, *Collector's Guide to American Wicker Furniture,* Hearst Books, NY, 1983

Saunders, Richard, *Wicker Furniture: A Guide to Restoring and Collecting,* Crown Publishing, NY 1976

Schwartz, Harry, *Rattan: Tropical Comfort Throughout the House,* Schiffer, PA, 1999

Scott, Tim, *Fine Wicker Furniture 1870-1930,* Schiffer, PA, 1990

Shixiang, Wang, *Classic Chinese Furniture,* Joint Publishing Co. Hong Kong, 1986

Shixiang, Wang, *Connoisseurship of Chinese Furniture,* Art Media Resources Ltd, 1990

Stephenson, Sue Honaker, *Rustic Furniture,* Van Nostrand Reinhold, NY, 1979

Stone, Joseph S., *Willow Chair How to Build Your Very Own,* Genesis Publications, CA, 1992

Sullivan, Michael, *The Arts of China,* University of California Press, Berkeley, 1984,

Thomas, Gertrude Z., *Richer than Spices,* Alfred A. Knopf, New York, 1972.

UNIDO, *Design and Manufacture of Bamboo and Rattan Furniture,* United Nations Industrial Development Organization, Vienna, 1996

van de Geijn-Verhoeven, Monique, et al., *Domestic Interiors at the Cape and in Batavia 1602-1795,* Wanders Publishers b.v., Zwolle, Gemeentemuseum, Den Haag, 2002

Watt, James C.Y., *The Sumptuous Basket – Chinese Lacquer with Basketry Panels,* China Institute of America, NY, 1985

Acknowledgments

A book like this cannot be researched, photographed and written without having a family who is willing to sacrifice its time together and pick up the slack that the author conveniently drops. I am indebted to my wife, Sher and my son, Andy, for their love, support, patience and sacrifices while I worked on this manuscript. Thank you from the bottom of my heart. Thanks to those great folks at The Caning Shop—Shelly, Jenny, Lerryn, and Tami—for covering for me while I photographed. Thanks to Jeff Miratello, Dennis Lee, and Chris Chan for providing the detailed photographs and numerous explanations of what occurs in the caning factories. Thanks to Stephen Siebert and David Hall for the wonderful photographs of the rattan harvesting and preparation in the jungle. I am grateful to Brian Crossley for his assistance with the history of caning and to Mei Han and Randy Raine-Reusch for translation of Chinese text. I owe a very special thanks to Andre Nigoghossian, for his endurance as a model and for his skill and technical abilities as a caner.

The Caning Shop's humble beginnings

INDEX

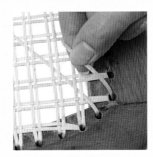

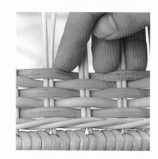